THE WEALTHY LIVING WORKBOOK

Simple Skills for Creating a Financially Fantastic Life

The Open Gate, LLC

Bethany Drosendahl

CONTENTS

WELCOME TO

THE OPEN GATE

...COME ON IN

FOUR STEPS
TO
WEALTHY LIVING

1. EXPLORE YOUR BELIEFS

2. DEVELOP YOUR SKILLS

3. CLARIFY YOUR VALUES

4. HONOR YOUR INTEGRITY

Do you want to experience a WEALTHY life?

This workbook is designed to empower and inspire you. Through an understanding of basic financial skills, you will thrive financially. It is not the amount of money you earn, but what you do with it that really counts. When you know you can create your own reality through mindful choices, you are truly free. This workbook will teach you to begin right where you are in the present moment. You will take responsibility for your choices in making money, spending money, saving money, and creating a healthy relationship with money. Finally, you will no longer pine for what you don't have, but start enjoying what you do have. When you recognize that you have a choice, "I can't afford it" becomes "That's not how I choose to spend my money".

Choice and responsibility
create freedom and power.

Along the way please remember:

$ If you have a strong reaction to an activity, instruction, or a specific area, pay attention to it. Your strong reaction is a clue to something you may want to look at on a deeper level.

$ Do not substitute someone else's opinion for your own.

$ Watch your language. Be careful of using dirty words; 'should', 'always', 'never', and 'can't'.

Whether you
think you can
or
you think you can't,
you're right!

~ Henry Ford

$\$^{+}$

Create a
Financially
Fantastic Life

ARE YOU READY...TO CREATE A FINANCIALLY FANTASTIC LIFE?

Time to set some intentions:

Please take a few minutes and a few deep breaths. When you are ready, write down what you would like to get out of this workbook.

You have brains in your head.
You have feet in your shoes.
You can steer yourself
Any direction you choose.

~ Dr. Seuss

$+

FOUR STEPS
TO
WEALTHY LIVING

Step 1:

EXPLORE YOUR BELIEFS

Building a Wealthy Life is like building a house…

You have to start with a good foundation.

$+

EXPLORE YOUR BELIEFS

9

EXPLORE YOUR BELIEFS

**Are you ready...
to become financially fit?**

Lets get started by discussing your current beliefs about money, wealth, and success. You may ask: why would I want to take time to explore these beliefs?

Simple: What you believe = what you think = how you behave = what you create. And what you want to create is a Wealthy Life!

Beliefs about money, wealth, and success come from one of two places. One is your Financial DNA – the ideas you inherited from your family of origin. The other is Cultural Myths – the ideas that are driven by society, pop culture, marketing, and collective activities. These beliefs float around in your environment like little blobs and they stick to you when you aren't paying attention.

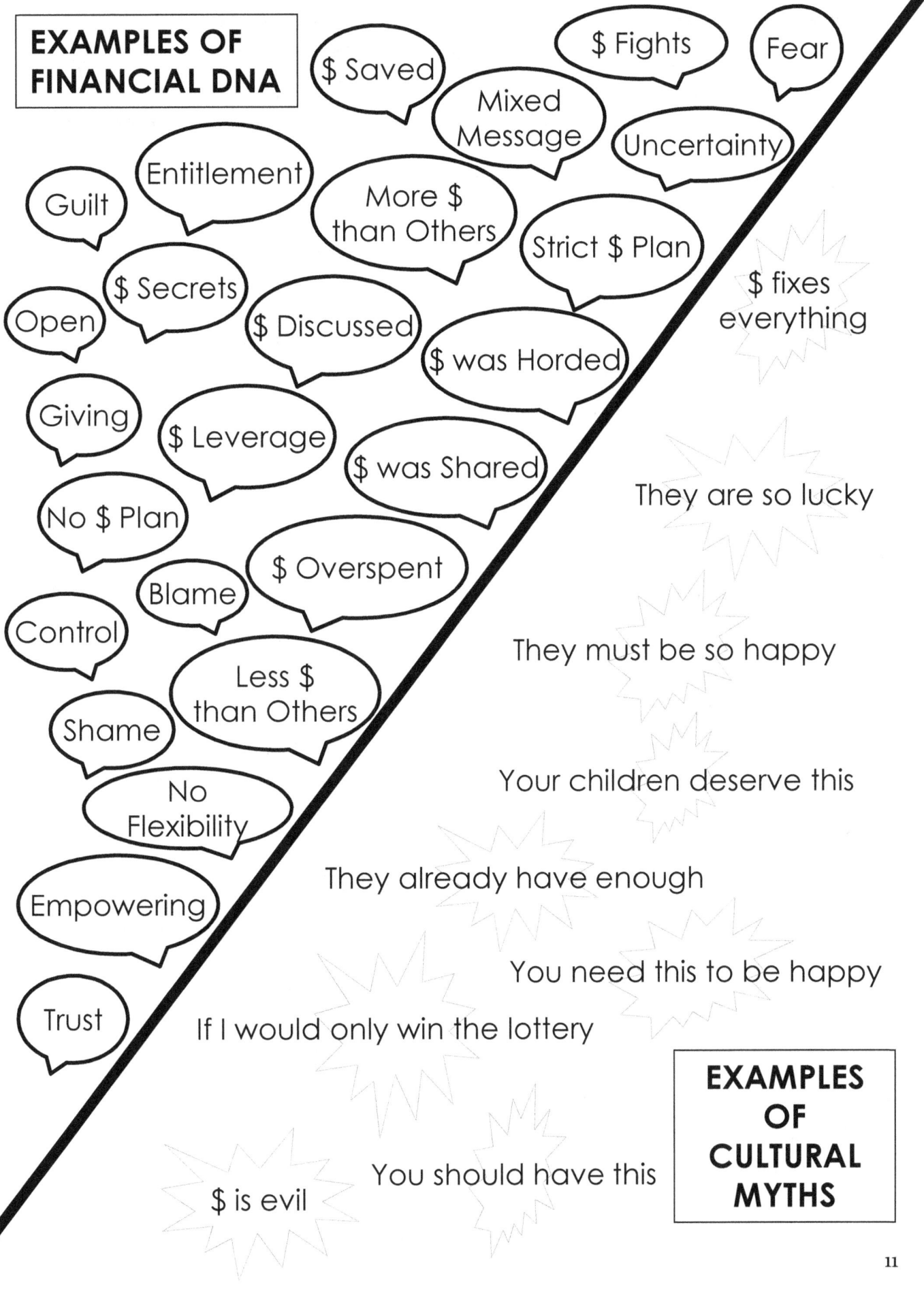

EXAMPLES OF FINANCIAL DNA

$ Saved

$ Fights

Fear

Mixed Message

Uncertainty

Entitlement

Guilt

More $ than Others

Strict $ Plan

$ Secrets

Open

$ Discussed

$ was Horded

Giving

$ Leverage

$ was Shared

No $ Plan

$ Overspent

Blame

Control

Less $ than Others

Shame

No Flexibility

Empowering

Trust

$ fixes everything

They are so lucky

They must be so happy

Your children deserve this

They already have enough

You need this to be happy

If I would only win the lottery

You should have this

$ is evil

EXAMPLES OF CULTURAL MYTHS

11

EXPLORE YOUR BELIEFS

Charting your current beliefs?

Settle in. Start to think about your checking account, your pay check, the cash in your pocket, paying your bills, getting the mail, etc. Think about the places and areas around your financial life.

When you are ready, start to write down on the next page what you are thinking- all the thoughts that pop into your head: memories of family experiences around money, current situations, etc. Write down what you think, how your body feels, and where in your body you are feeling the emotions. Don't censor yourself and don't judge.

Now go through the list and circle items on the sheet related to your Financial DNA. Box items related to Cultural Myths.

You have just discovered some of your current beliefs about Wealthy Living. Congratulate yourself. Drink a glass of water and be kind to yourself. Wealthy Living is 70% thought and 30% skill.

EXPLORE YOUR BELIEFS

So now what?

For each of these **beliefs** you can ask yourself:

$ Is it true?

$ Is it working for me?

For the **beliefs** that you answer NO to, those **beliefs** are no longer serving you. Take a good look at your **old beliefs** and thank them. If you just try to say, 'well, I won't think that anymore,' it will just keep popping up on you. What we resist, persists. So what you want to do is replace your **old, tired, worn-out beliefs** with **shiny new beliefs**.

The next page will help you with this process.

REMEMBER: If you take a thought out, you want to replace it with a new thought. DO NOT focus on not having the thought– that will just give it more attention!

OLD BELIEFS	**NEW BELIEFS**
1.	1.
2.	2.
3.	3.
4.	4.
5.	5.
6.	6.
7.	7.
8.	8.

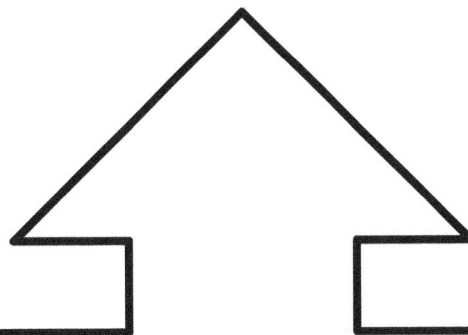

Directions: Pick eight **beliefs** from the previous page. Write these under **OLD BELIEFS** above. Write your **NEW BELIEFS** in the next column. "I can't" becomes "I can"; "In the past I..." becomes "In the present I..."; "I worry about..." becomes "I am open to..."; "I am stressed about..." becomes "I am excited about..."; "I blame" becomes "I forgive"; "I shouldn't" becomes "I choose".

Look for the opportunities in every situation.

HEY, Watch your language!!
'*I'm broke*'...YEEK!
How about...
'*That is not how I choose to spend my money*'
...now that is empowering!

$+

EXPLORE YOUR BELIEFS

WEALTHY LIVING

This next exercise will help align your thinking with your desire for **Wealthy Living**.

$ **Old Beliefs** create resistance.

$ When you seek something you believe is missing from your life, you are searching outside of yourself.

$ Searching outside of yourself leads you on a fruitless chase and possibly a financially destructive one.

$ You are focusing on what you **believe** you are lacking, which attracts more of what you don't want.

$ This leads to **habits** that are not in alignment with **Wealthy Living**.

Provided you maintain the conditions which make it possible, you can create anything.

EXPLORE YOUR BELIEFS

ARE YOU WEALTHY?

Settle in. Find a thought, a moment, a smell, a color, something that is your happy space, place, item. On the next page write down all the ways you are:

$ **LOVED, LOVABLE, LOVING**

$ **HAPPY, JOYOUS**

$ **FULFILLED**

$ **GRATEFUL, BLESSED**

$ **ENRICHED, BOUNTIFUL**

$ **A CHILD OF GOD (A HIGHER POWER OF YOUR CHOICE)**

Take a moment and take this all in. How does it feel in your body, mind, and emotions when you see all the wonderful things about your life?

You have this **WEALTH** in your life **RIGHT NOW!**

THIS IS WEALTHY LIVING

THIS IS YOU AND YOU ARE THIS

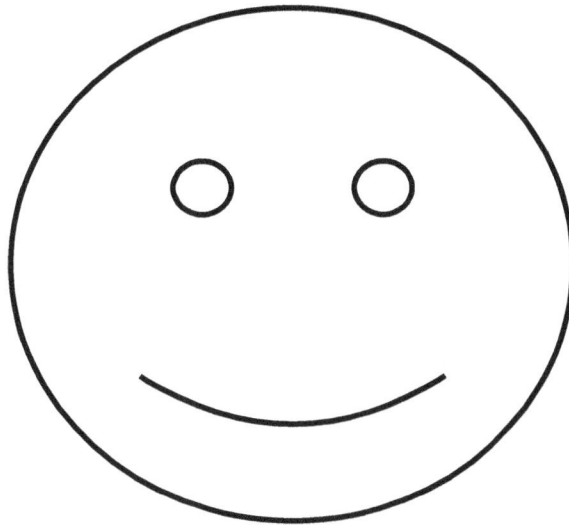

WRITE DOWN ALL THE WAYS THAT YOU ARE:

LOVED   HAPPY   GRATEFUL   FULFILLED   ENRICHED

EXPLORE YOUR BELIEFS

You have this **WEALTH** in your life

RIGHT NOW!

From the exercise on the previous page, look at the abundant supply of **WEALTH** that you are right now.

Are you ready to claim it?

If you are ready, then claim it!

Answer '**YES, I AM!**' on the next page.

If you are not ready, no judgment.

Just know it is always waiting for you.

REMEMBER:

Change your perception +

change your thinking +

change your habits =

change your reality

ARE YOU WEALTHY?

EXPLORE YOUR BELIEFS

QUESTION: HOW DO YOU BECOME GOOD AT SOMETHING?

ANSWER: PRACTICE, PRACTICE, PRACTICE

HOMEWORK(APPLAUSE HERE)

$ Be grateful

$ Recognize the **Wealth Living** that you have right now

$ Stay aware of what you are thinking/telling yourself when you are: Shopping, at the bank, paying bills, getting the mail, answering the phone, or any activity that may be associated with your money

$ Write down any strong emotions/how your body feels

$ Write down what you are telling yourself

$ Challenge that thought...is it true?

$ Be kind to yourself, no judgment!

$ Develop replacement thoughts as needed

UNDERSTAND

MONEY = Energy = Current

MONEY is neither good nor bad

MONEY is simply a means of exchange

EXPLORE YOUR BELIEFS

BELIEFS CREATE HABITS

$ Your emotions are clues

$ How does your financial situation make you physically feel?

$ Tight-shouldered, sick to your stomach, and frustrated, or happy, free, and joyful?

$ Recognize the signs

$ What do you do to handle those feelings?

$ How do you react?

$ These are the **habits** that form around your beliefs

$ **Habits** are outward expressions of your inner beliefs

REMEMBER: Push yourself outside of your safety zone, and challenge your old beliefs. Making this change on the inside will change your outer behaviors, moving you toward **Wealthy Living**. Expand your **Wealthy Living** by **believing** you are **wealthy right now,** recognizing how that feels, and behaving 'as if' you are by DEVELOPING YOUR SKILLS.

24

Where are you right now? You need to start from where you are right here, right now.

$+

EXPLORE YOUR BELIEFS

FOUR STEPS
TO
WEALTHY LIVING

Step 2:

DEVELOP YOUR SKILLS

Whether you
think you can
or
you think you can't,
you're right!

~ Henry Ford

$\$^{+}$

DEVELOP
YOUR
SKILLS

DEVELOP YOUR SKILLS

One minute after you turn sixteen, someone comes to you and hands you a set of car keys. Here you are, now off you go.

Getting a driver's license is an American right of passage. I remember getting mine. Even today, it reminds me of **FREEDOM AND EMPOWERMENT**. I felt **FREE AND EMPOWERED**.

BUT, someone had to teach me how to drive a car, and what the rules are. I had to practice. But what if you were not taught? You might have arrived at your destination, or you might not have arrived at your destination. It probably would have been a **FEARFUL** ride, full of **UNCERTAINTY**.

MANAGING YOUR $ IS LIKE THIS: If you never learned the skills to manage your $, you probably don't have a plan. When you don't have a plan for your $, it is a **FEARFUL** ride full of **UNCERTAINTY**.

$* RESPONSIBILITY & CHOICE *$

=

$* FREEDOM & EMPOWERMENT *$

DEVELOP YOUR SKILLS

HOW MUCH MONEY WILL YOU MANAGE OVER YOUR LIFETIME?

The average American will manage approximately $5,000,000 over their lifetime. **YES, I AM TALKING TO YOU!** Yes, school teachers, office workers, health care workers. Regular people. The people sitting next to you at the coffee shop. The person working on your car. The meter maid that just gave you a parking ticket. The person you see in the mirror every morning. It's OK that most people don't think of their $ this way. **BUT YOU WILL MANAGE APPROXIMATELY $5,000,000 OVER YOUR LIFETIME.**

SO WHAT ARE YOU GOING TO CREATE WITH YOUR $5,000,000?

PLEASE NOTE: I do give you permission to make that number as big as you like. Think of it as the first floor on which you can create a skyscraper!

NO SKILLS/NO PLAN

DON'T BUILD YOUR FINANCIAL LIFE ON THIS FOUNDATION!

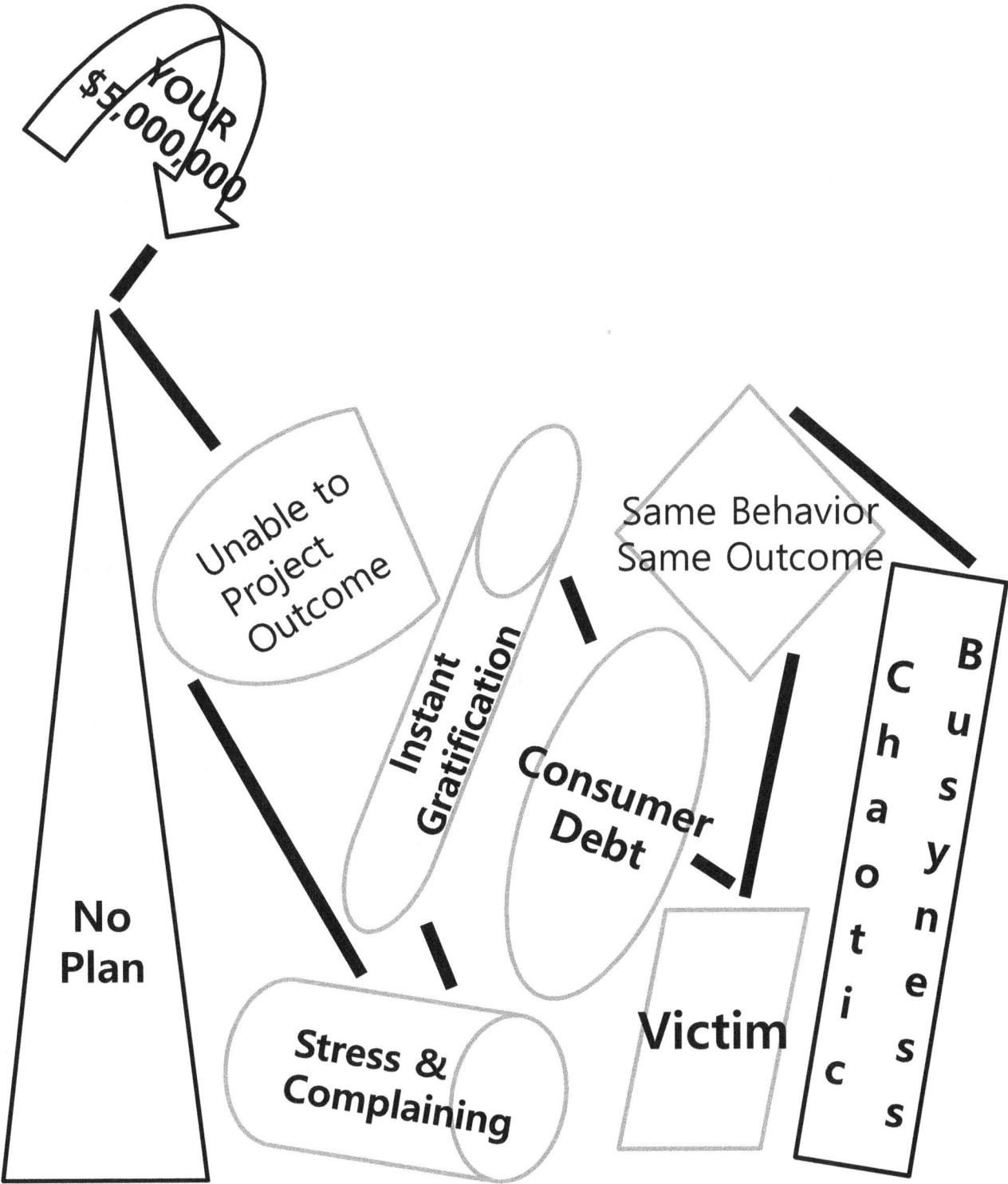

YOUR $5,000,000

Unable to Project Outcome

Same Behavior Same Outcome

Instant Gratification

Consumer Debt

No Plan

Stress & Complaining

Victim

Chaotic

Busyness

NO SKILLS/NO PLAN

DON'T BUILD YOUR FINANCIAL LIFE ON THIS FOUNDATION!

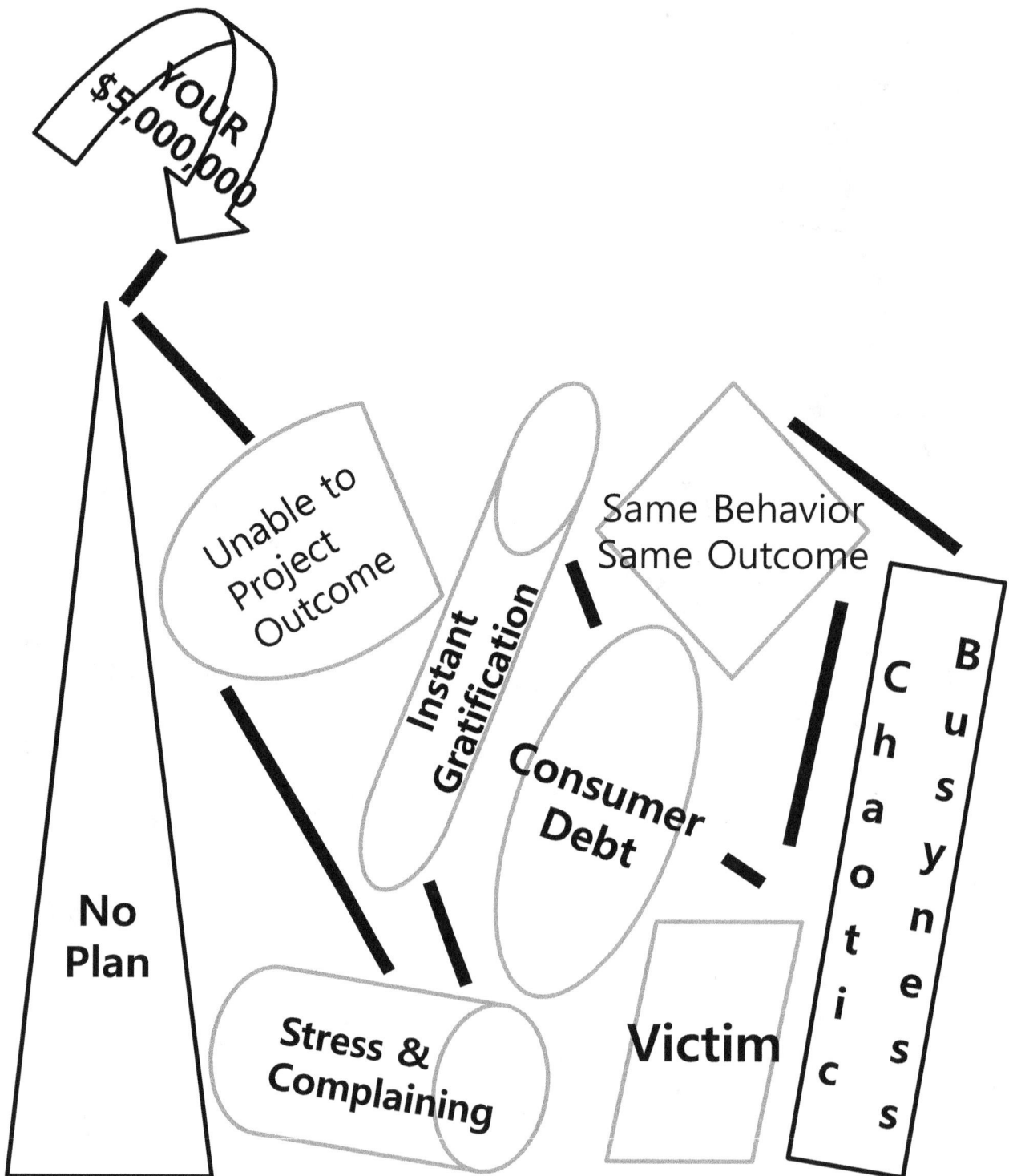

YOUR $5,000,000

Unable to Project Outcome

Same Behavior Same Outcome

Instant Gratification

Consumer Debt

No Plan

Stress & Complaining

Victim

Chaotic

Busyness

NO SKILLS/NO PLAN

The following contains no judgment-it is only an observation. **The details of the stories vary, but the underlying traits, behaviors, and beliefs do not.**

NO PLAN for your $ leads to being **UNABLE TO PROJECT OUTCOMES**. For instance, your insurance is due every six months but there is a panic when the bill arrives. No money to pay the bill. Car needs new tires; Refrigerator stops working; Christmas arrives every December...This panic and uncertainty creates **STRESS** and leads to **COMPLAINING**. The **STRESS** leads to habits which sooth the situation = **INSTANT GRATIFICATION**. 'I work hard', 'I deserve it', etc. **INSTANT GRATIFICATION** leads to **CONSUMER DEBT. CONSUMER DEBT** consumes your $. It is a financial tumor. Go out and charge a nice dinner. Your body will process that meal within 24 hours, however, making minimum payments, it will take you approximately 6 months to pay for it and will cost you an extra 12% (that is approximately the same amount of $ as a lunch out or 5 coffees)! Chronic **CONSUMER DEBT** leads to a **VICTIM** MENTALITY. A **VICTIM** MENTALITY = wanting things to be different but focusing only on the current situation. Every time one of those bills shows up, you feel guilty about the past and worry about the future and use your money in the present to pay. It feels like it is being done to you: "Poor me, I can't catch a break, I have the worst luck." The cycle continues until you are officially broken. Broken people perform the **SAME BEHAVIOR** and expect different outcomes. **SAME BEHAVIOR = SAME OUTCOME.** Broken people have very **CHAOTIC** lives (think **UNABLE TO PROJECT OUTCOMES**) full of **BUSYNESS,** but they never really produce anything. Broken people are too busy to change, to learn something new, or to make time to create a plan.

WHAT IS TRUE: Without a PLAN you will wake up at 50 having earned half of your $5,000,000, and you will have little or nothing to show for it. You will have a 'HOLY CRAP' moment, and most likely all you will have created for yourself is a hot mess.

$^+

DEVELOP YOUR SKILLS

DEVELOP YOUR SKILLS

HAVE NO FEAR!

Take a few deep breaths. Drink a big glass of water.

BECAUSE The skills you need to create a **PLAN** are simple, there are only three parts to your $ and only three skills for you to learn and master.

O.K. LET'S GET STARTED!

For the next exercise you will need some colored pens, pencils, crayons, or markers, or you can just use your finger and follow the directions. (HA! You thought I was going to give you an excuse not to start. NO EXCUSES. **YOU CAN DO THIS**!!)

REMEMBER: The three things you must do to succeed:
$ PRACTICE $, $ PRACTICE $, $ PRACTICE $

HOW TO BUILD A FINANCIAL FOUNDATION

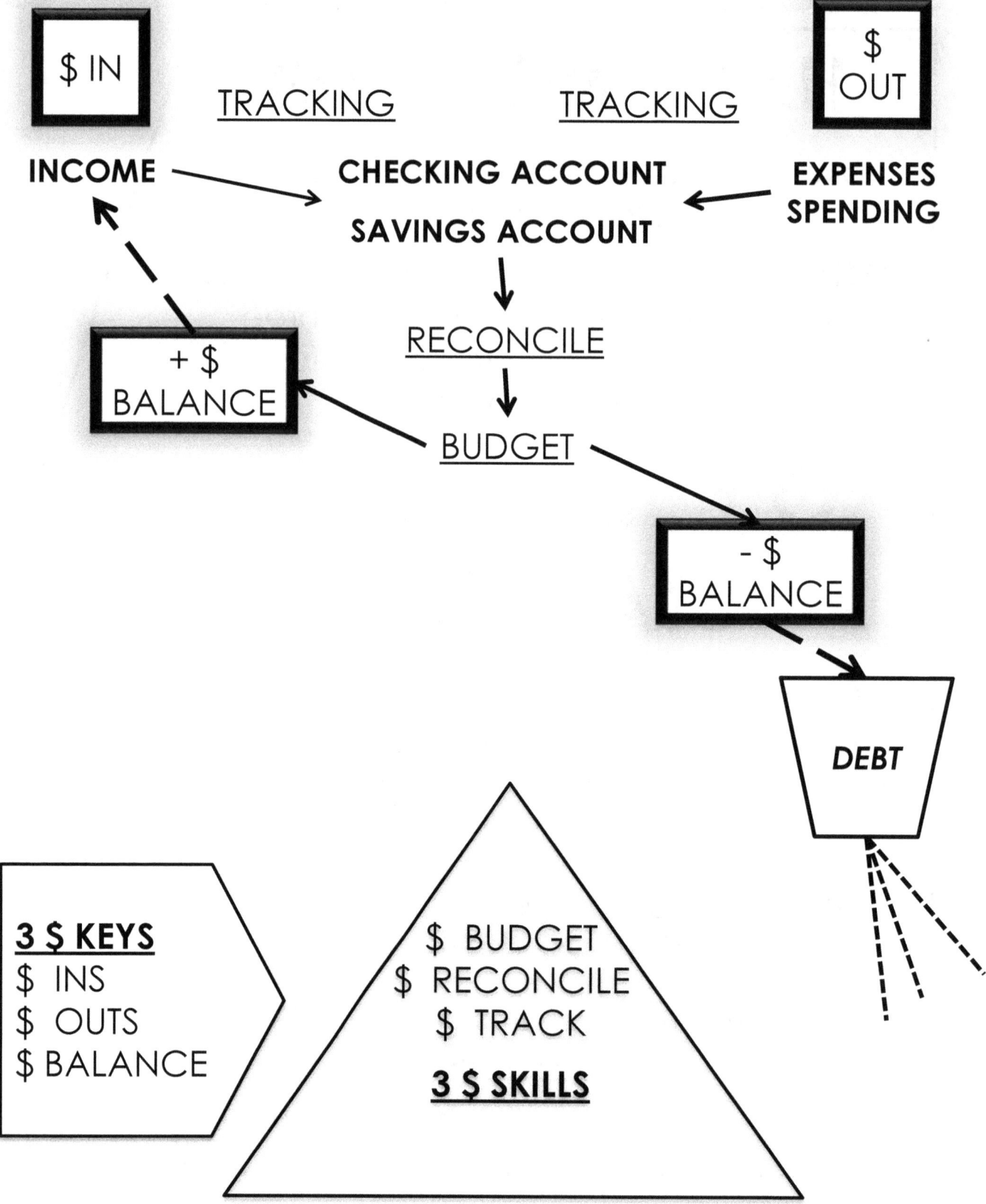

$ IN

TRACKING   TRACKING

$ OUT

INCOME → CHECKING ACCOUNT ← EXPENSES SPENDING

SAVINGS ACCOUNT

RECONCILE

+ $ BALANCE ← BUDGET → - $ BALANCE

DEBT

3 $ KEYS
$ INS
$ OUTS
$ BALANCE

$ BUDGET
$ RECONCILE
$ TRACK

3 $ SKILLS

HOW TO BUILD A FINANCIAL FOUNDATION

$ There are only three keys to your money: **INS**, **OUTS**, **BALANCE**

$ There are only three skills to master: **TRACKING**, **RECONCILING**, **BUDGETING**

OK, LET'S GET STARTED: We will start with the **INS**. The INS is all **$** that comes in. We will call this **INCOME**. Take your pen, pencil, marker, crayon, finger and circle the word **INCOME**. Now follow the arrow to **TRACKING**. **TRACKING** is your first skill. **TRACKING** is bringing awareness and attention to your **$**. Down in the pyramid, next to **TRACKING**, write "**AWARENESS; ATTENTION**". In this case you are **TRACKING** the **INS**. Now you need a place to put your **INS**. This is your **CHECKING ACCOUNT** and **SAVINGS ACCOUNT**. Make a figure eight around the **CHECKING ACCOUNT** and **SAVINGS ACCOUNT**. Then make a circle around both. Pencils down. **CHECKING ACCOUNTS** and **SAVINGS ACCOUNTS** are receptacles. Places to hold your **$**. Now go over to the **OUTS**. This is the second part of your **$**. Notice that there are two types of **OUTS**. **EXPENSES** are what you spend your **$** on to stay alive: a clean, safe place to live, utilities, food, and transportation. **SPENDING** is what you choose to spend your **$** on to enrich your life. Pencils ready. Circle **EXPENSES** and **SPENDING**. Now follow the arrow past TRACKING back to your **CHECKING ACCOUNT** and **SAVING ACCOUNT**. Pencils down. You are **TRACKING** (**AWARENESS; ATTENTION**) your **EXPENSES** and **SPENDING**.

Great Job! Flip the page to continue...

HOW TO BUILD A FINANCIAL FOUNDATION

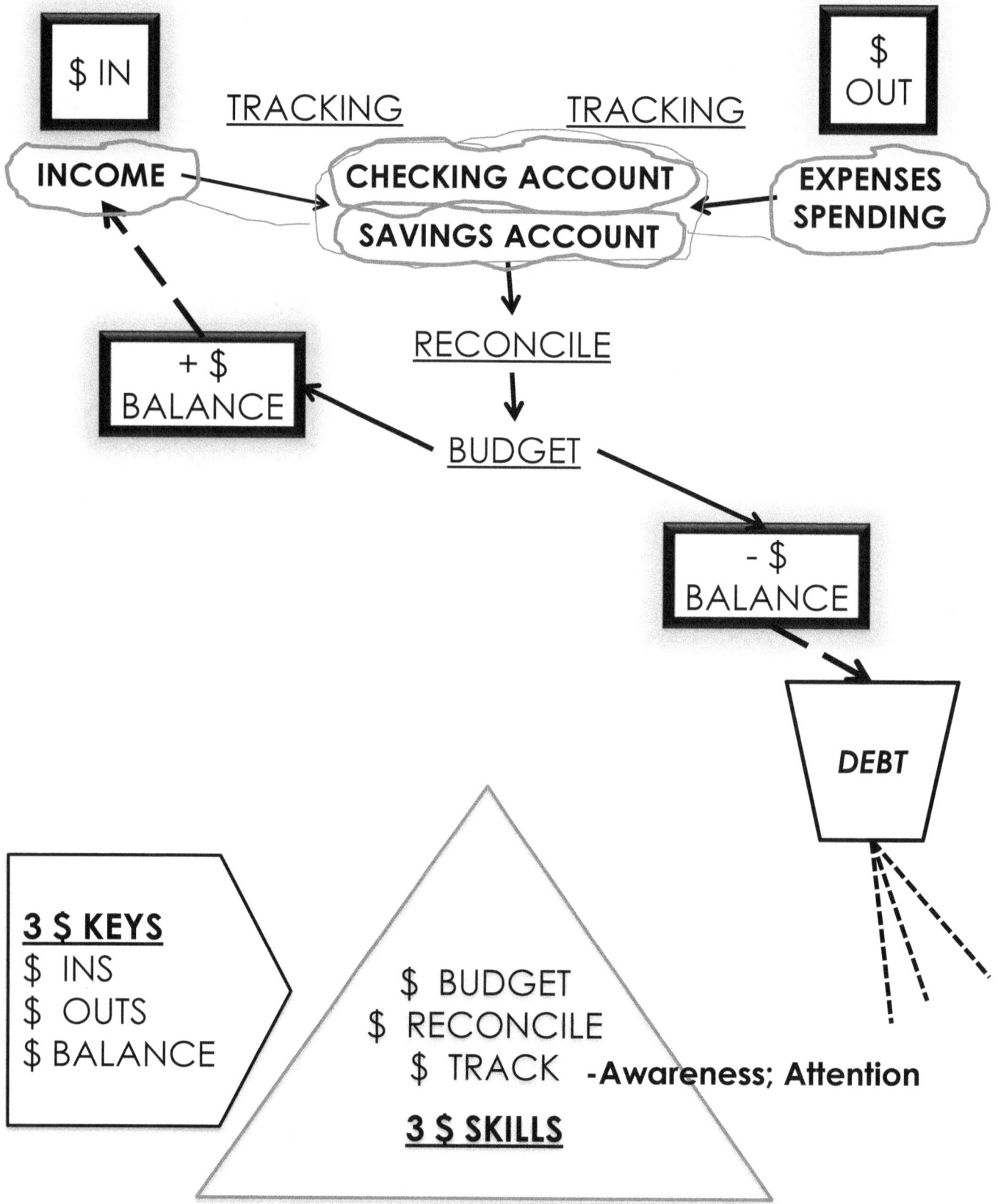

$ IN

$ OUT

TRACKING   TRACKING

INCOME → CHECKING ACCOUNT ← EXPENSES SPENDING

SAVINGS ACCOUNT

RECONCILE

+ $ BALANCE

BUDGET

- $ BALANCE

DEBT

3 $ KEYS
$ INS
$ OUTS
$ BALANCE

$ BUDGET
$ RECONCILE
$ TRACK   -Awareness; Attention

3 $ SKILLS

HOW TO BUILD A FINANCIAL FOUNDATION

OK, HERE WE GO: You are now **TRACKING** your **INS** and **OUTS** into your **CHECKING** and **SAVINGS ACCOUNT**. Time for your second skill. To **RECONCILE** is to bring awareness, attention, and alignment to your $. Down in the pyramid next to **RECONCILE** write "**AWARENESS; ATTENTION; ALIGNMENT**". Now draw a thick arrow down from your **CHECKING AND SAVINGS ACCOUNT** to the word **BUDGET**. Under the word **BUDGET** write "**$ PLAN**". Notice that **BUDGET** is the third skill. Down in the pyramid next to **BUDGET** write "**THE PLAN; THE HOW**". Great! Now let's tie it all together. Circle **BUDGET**. When you are in alignment with your **BUDGET**, your **BALANCE** will be positive. Draw a line from your **BUDGET** to **+ BALANCE**. If you are not in alignment with your **BUDGET**, your **BALANCE** will be negative. Draw a line from your **BUDGET** to **– BALANCE**.

GREAT JOB! FLIP THE PAGE TO CONTINUE...

HOW TO BUILD A FINANCIAL FOUNDATION

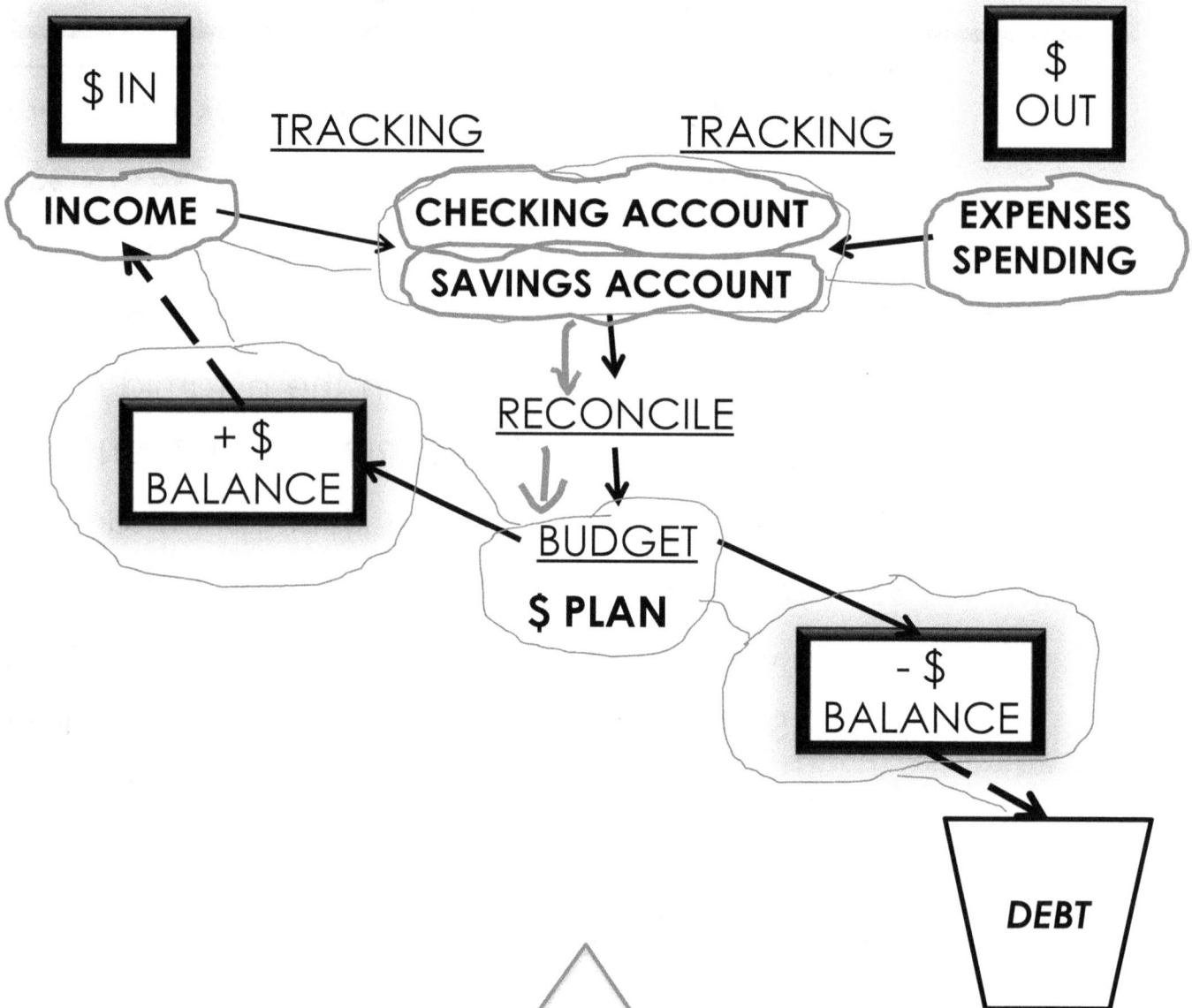

$ IN

TRACKING   TRACKING

INCOME

CHECKING ACCOUNT

SAVINGS ACCOUNT

$ OUT

EXPENSES SPENDING

+ $ BALANCE

RECONCILE

BUDGET

$ PLAN

- $ BALANCE

DEBT

3 $ KEYS
$ INS
$ OUTS
$ BALANCE

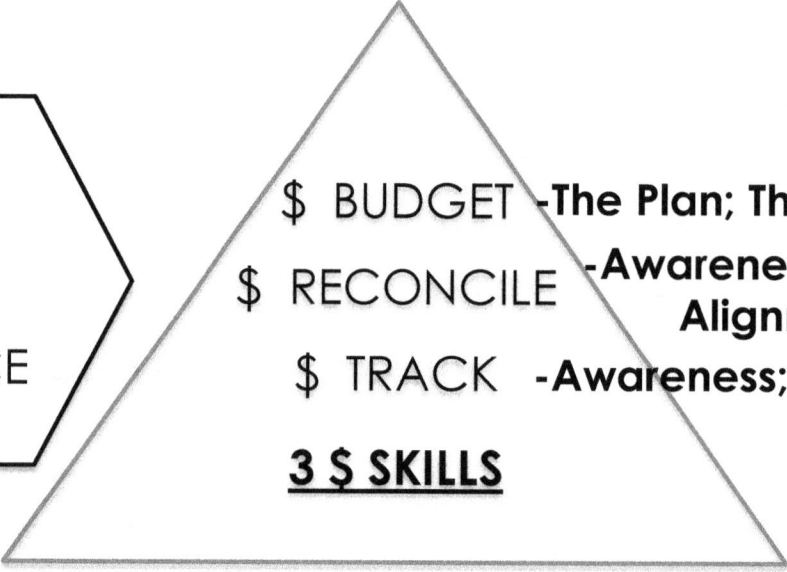

$ BUDGET -The Plan; The How

$ RECONCILE -Awareness; Attention; Alignment

$ TRACK -Awareness; Attention

3 $ SKILLS

HOW TO BUILD A
FINANCIAL FOUNDATION

It's a little messy, right? That's OK. Have you ever seen a construction site? It looks like a big old mess while the foundation is being put in. But without a good foundation the building won't stand for long. Depending on where you are right now with your **$**, you are going to go through a bit of a mess when you start building your new foundation. I promise that it will be worth it.

HOW TO BUILD A FINANCIAL FOUNDATION

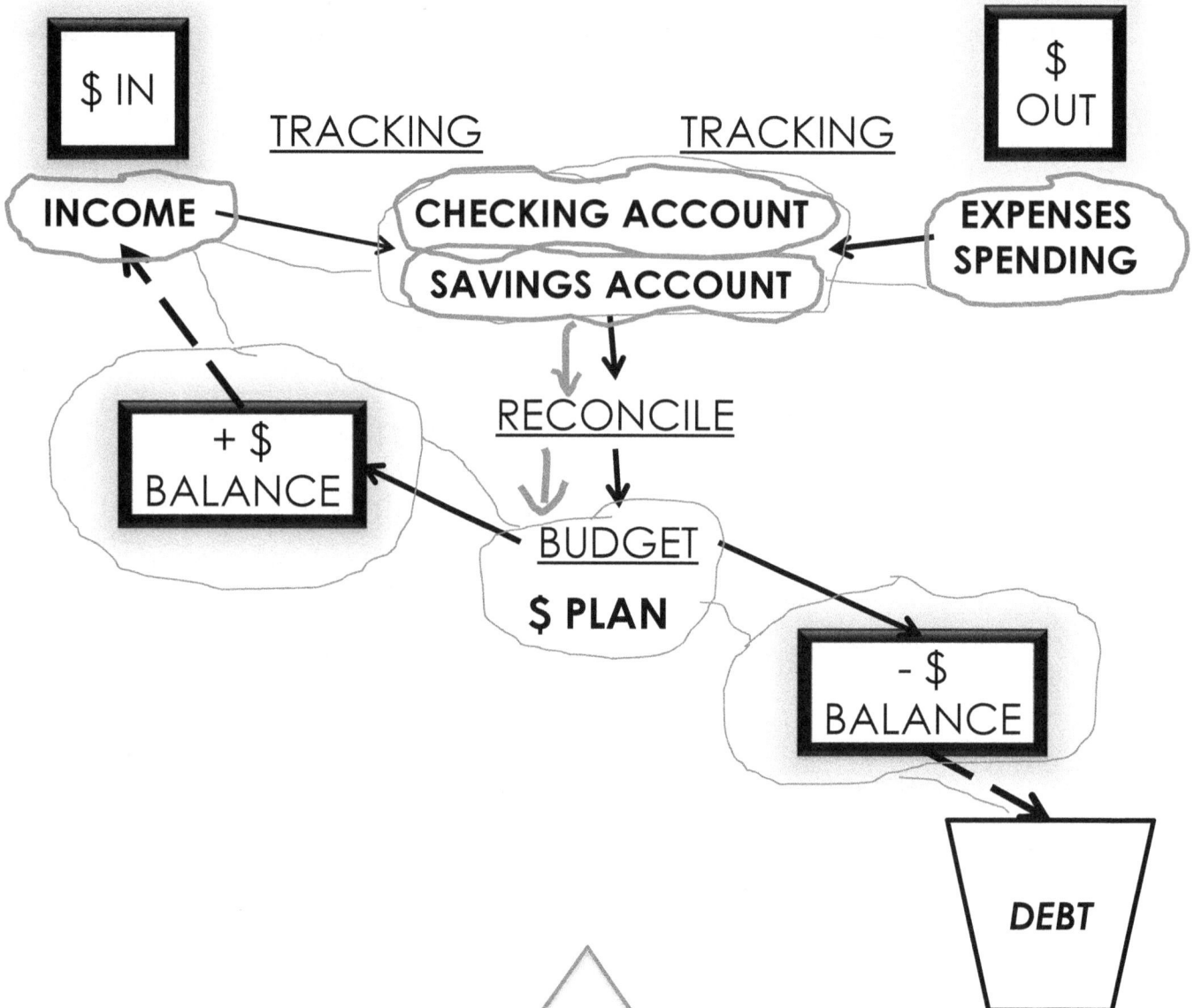

$ IN

$ OUT

TRACKING   TRACKING

INCOME

CHECKING ACCOUNT

SAVINGS ACCOUNT

EXPENSES
SPENDING

RECONCILE

+ $
BALANCE

BUDGET

$ PLAN

- $
BALANCE

DEBT

3 $ KEYS
$ INS
$ OUTS
$ BALANCE

$ BUDGET -The Plan; The How

$ RECONCILE -Awareness; Attention;
Alignment

$ TRACK -Awareness; Attention

3 $ SKILLS

HOW TO BUILD A FINANCIAL FOUNDATION

LETS REVIEW:

$ There are only three keys to your money: **INS, OUTS, BALANCE**

$ There are only three skills to master: **TRACKING, RECONCILING, BUDGETING**

$ Make the **INS** as big as possible

$ Make the **OUTS** as small as possible

$ The **BALANCE** is the difference between the **INS** and the **OUTS**

$ The **BUDGET** is your plan for your $

$ When you **TRACK** your $ in and out of your **CHECKING AND SAVINGS ACCOUNT**, you are bringing awareness and attention to your $

$ When you **RECONCILE** your **INS** and **OUTS** to your **BUDGET**, your **PLAN**, you are bringing awareness and attention to how you are using your $

$ When the way you use your $ is in alignment with your **BUDGET**, your **PLAN**, then your **BALANCE** will be positive

$ When you are not in alignment with your **BUDGET**, your **PLAN**, then your balance will be negative

$ If you consistently have a negative **BALANCE** you will accumulate **DEBT**. We have discussed **DEBT**. Just remember, accumulating **DEBT** is like trying to drink out of a cup with a hole in the bottom...no fun!

$ You want a positive **BALANCE**. This is what allows you to **LIVE WEALTHY** and **BUILD YOUR FINANCIAL FOUNDATION**. It allows you to have more choices.

DEVELOP YOUR SKILLS

REMEMBER YOUR $5,000,000?

IT IS TIME TO HAVE A

PLAN

The starting point is a

BUDGET

This is the PLAN for your MONEY

A **BUDGET** is a starting point. A **BUDGET** is a changing, growing document. **BUDGETING** is a skill!

$* LETS BUDGET *$

Where are you right now?
You need to start from
where you are right here,
right now.

$⁺

DEVELOP
YOUR
SKILLS

DEVELOP YOUR SKILLS

On the pages that follow are four sample budgets. These budgets are supplied as guides to build your own unique budget. Just as no two people are alike, no two budgets are alike. In fact, your own budget will change as you and your life change. That is why it is called a changing, growing document. It will become a road map of your journey. One important point is that you have to start where you are right now and work your way to where you want to be.

The pyramid on the next page shows the progress of this journey. WARNING: you will have to work with numbers.

No worries, keep it simple.

This is not a step you can skip and hope to be successful. All financially healthy people budget in some form. There is no magical pill to get you out of this.

This is a skill you must master to master **WEALTHY LIVING**.

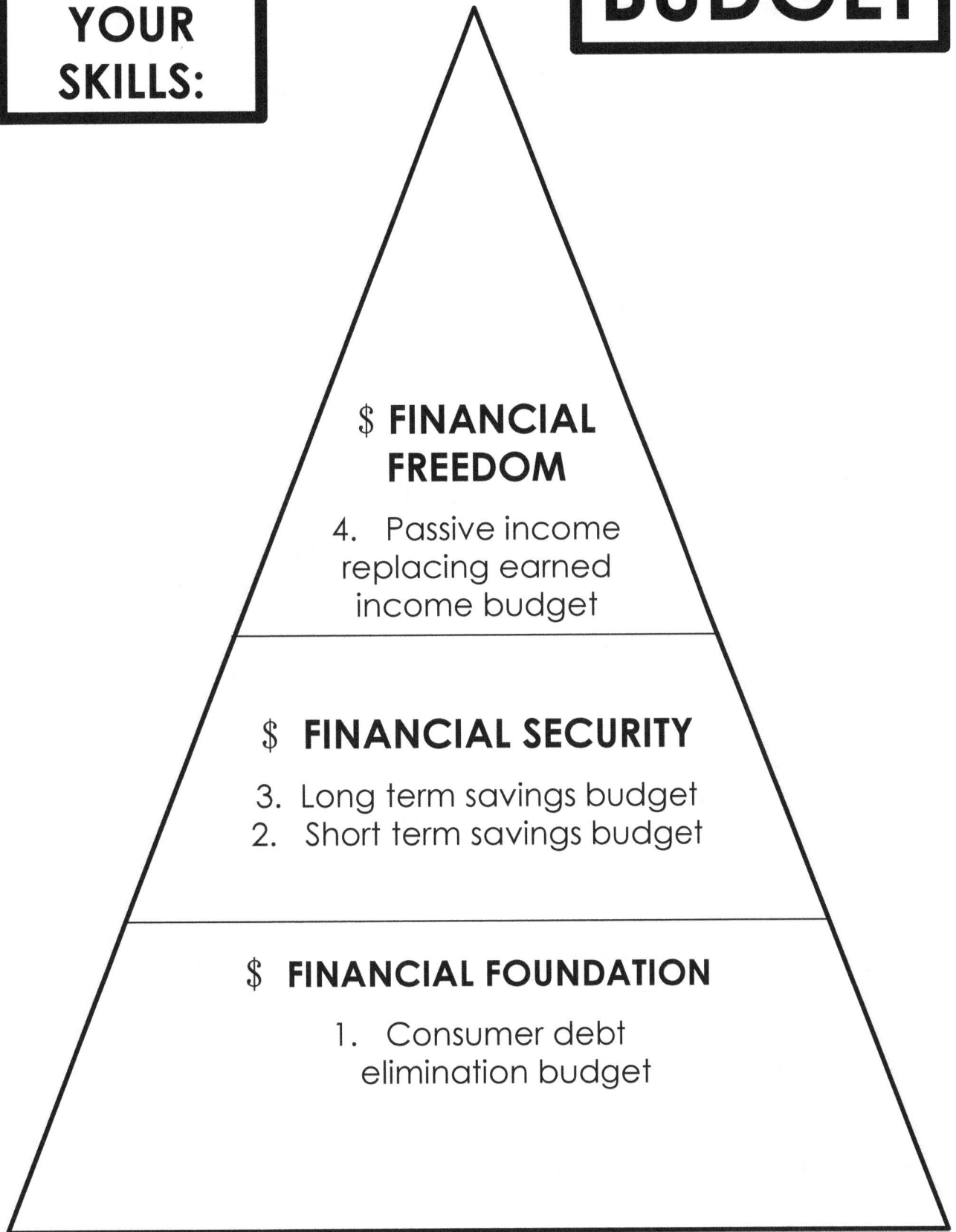

BUDGET

$ **FINANCIAL
FREEDOM**

4. Passive income
replacing earned
income budget

$ **FINANCIAL SECURITY**

3. Long term savings budget
2. Short term savings budget

$ **FINANCIAL FOUNDATION**

1. Consumer debt
elimination budget

Budgeting ~ Keep It Simple!

$ First and most important, "**Budget**" is a verb; it is an action word. You must take action.

Remember: You eat an elephant one bite at a time.

$ You can use a computer spreadsheet that you create, you can use an app or other software program, or you can use a notebook, pencil, and calculator. But regardless of what you use, you must do the work.

Remember: Start from where you are right now.

$ Make a date with yourself (and your partner if you have one) for one hour every week. Be consistent and stay committed. Sundays work well for a lot of people. At first this may seem like a chore but it is really a privilege. You are creating your **WEALTHY LIVING** habits! So light some candles, put on some good music, and enjoy getting your budget on.

Remember: Celebrate after you complete your hour!

$ Speaking of partners, do you keep your finances separate or do you join your funds together? Appendix 2, 'To Comingle or Not to Comingle Funds?, That is the Question.' (Page 183), contains questions to consider.

Remember: Whatever you do, make a conscious choice.

Skills To Master

$ **Daily** – Track Expenses

$ **Monthly** – Balance Checkbook

$ **Monthly** – Reconcile Actual Spending

to Budget

$ **Every three months**– Adjust Budget Estimates

$ **Get Income Up**

$ **Eliminate or Reduce Expenses/Spending**

$ **Yearly** – Review Year

and Create New Budget

$ **As Needed** – Seek Help

$ **As Needed** – Celebrate Successes

Budgeting ~ The Basics

The columns

The first column: Income (The INS), Expense (The OUTS), and BALANCE

$ At the very top will be the **INS.** This is the amount of money that you have to spend from all sources.

$ Please take a moment to look at your pay stub. The amount you earn is your Gross Pay. Then you will have deductions – taxes, insurance, taxes (this is not a typo). Gross pay less your deductions equals your funds available.

$ Next come the **OUTS.** The expenses are grouped in general categories: Home, Transportation, Health, Food, and Other.

$ Your **INS** less your **OUTS** equals your **BALANCE.** A positive balance means you are spending less than you make. A negative balance means you are spending more than you make.

Budgeting ~ The Basics

The columns

The second column: Yearly Budget

$ The **Yearly Budget** is simply your **Monthly Budget** multiplied by 12 (months).

The third column: Monthly Budget

$ This is your estimate of all your **monthly expenses**. Please note as an example, if you pay $600 for your insurance once every six months, you will budget $100 a month. ($600/6 months equals $100 a month). This is important. If you follow your budget, you will have $600 to pay your bill!

The fourth column: Actuals

$ You input/write in how much you actually spend. Hint, there is not a line on your budget that is marked 'other' or 'miscellaneous'.

The fifth column: Differences

$ This column is a calculation. Math time! Take your monthly estimate (column 3) less what you actually spent (column 4) and this equals your **Differences**.

Budgeting ~ The Basics

The rows

The INS

$ Budget for the amount of money you actually have to spend.

$ If you have three jobs and receive three pay checks, list each one separately.

The OUTS

$ Expenses are grouped by category.

$ Additional rows can be added, but be careful! If you have a three page budget...you have an issue.

Now pick a sample **Budget** based on where you are financially right now...

Budgeting ~ The Basics

Let's get started on a basic budget.

For this exercise, we are going to use the following assumptions and keep it simple:

$ We will start with a **Debt Reduction Budget**. What this means is any extra money left over at the end of the month goes to paying down consumer debt.

$ We are going to assume that bills and income occur in even amounts each month of the year. Individual circumstances will vary depending on your situation. Income can vary from month to month for a variety of reasons but this assumption will keep it simple.

The following page has our example **Debt Elimination Budget**. First look at the template, then we will walk through the steps to complete one of these.

Consumer Debt Elimination Budget

%		Yearly Budget	Monthly Budget	Jan Actual	Difference
	INCOME				
	Income	$	$	$	$
	Other Income	$	$	$	$
	TOTAL INCOME	$	$	$	$
	EXPENSE				
	Mortgage/Rent	$	$	$	$
	Utilities	$	$	$	$
	Garbage	$	$	$	$
	Cable/Internet	$	$	$	$
	Cell Phone	$	$	$	$
	Insurance	$	$		
	House Maintenance	$	$	$	$
	Car Loan	$	$	$	$
	Car Insurance	$	$	$	$
	Car Maintenance	$	$	$	$
	Gas	$	$	$	$
	Life Insurance	$	$	$	$
	Deductible	$	$	$	$
	Prescriptions	$	$	$	$
	Groceries	$	$	$	$
	Debt	$	$	$	$
	Debt	$	$	$	$
	Debt	$	$	$	$
	Kid's Stuff	$	$	$	$
	Pet Stuff	$	$	$	$
	Hair	$	$	$	$
	Clothing	$	$	$	$
	Allowance	$	$	$	$
	TOTAL EXPENSES	$	$	$	$
	BALANCE	$	$	$	$

55

Consumer Debt Elimination Budget Highlights

Step #1

Determine what you expect your income to be. Let's break this down in pieces:

$ Start with your current paycheck. This is where you are today. Increasing this amount will help, but start with where you are.

$ Determine how much your actual take-home pay comes to. This is your gross pay, after deductions. Let's keep it simple by using these figures. We'll assume a gross pay of $70,000 annually but $10,000 of deductions. This leaves us with an annual take home pay of $60,000. Since we are spreading this evenly over 12 months – each month take home pay equals $5,000 ($60,000 divided by 12 months)

The following page shows us what this looks like:

Budgeting Basics - Income

	Yearly Budget	Monthly Budget
INCOME		
Income	$ 60,000.00	$ 5,000.00
Other Income	$	$
TOTAL INCOME	$	$

$ You can see our annual take home pay of $60,000 and our monthly budget for $5,000.

$ We will come back to the actual amounts in a bit.

Budgeting Basics - Expenses

Step #2

Determine what you expect your expenses to be.

There is a lot to be covered in this section so let's start with the big ticket items:

$ We will begin with items that are tough to change – car loan and mortgage or rent. You probably know what this is each month so dig out your last loan payment or rent bill and be ready to fill this in.

$ While we are on home and car, look up your past 3 months of utility, cable, internet, cell phone, and insurance bills. Take an average of the past 3 months and let's fill those in.

We are going to use some typical figures on the following pages to give us a sense of what it looks like. Your numbers will be different so it's important to review your actual expenses and have realistic numbers.

Budgeting Basics - Expenses

EXPENSE	Yearly Budget	Monthly Budget
Mortgage/Rent	$ 9,600.00	$ 800.00
Utilities	$ 2,400.00	$ 200.00
Garbage	$ 600.00	$ 50.00
Cable/Internet	$ 1,200.00	$ 100.00
Cell Phone	$ 1,200.00	$ 100.00
Insurance	$ 1,200.00	$ 100.00
House Maintenance	$ 1,200.00	$ 100.00
Car Loan	$ 5,400.00	$ 450.00
Car Insurance	$ 1,500.00	$ 125.00

Notes:
$ If you pay rent, you will not need house maintenance, but you will need renters insurance.
$ Your home owner's insurance will most likely be included in your mortgage.

$ In this case, determine your monthly figures and let the annual amount be calculated by multiplying the monthly amount by 12.

$ Let's take a look at more expenses.

Budgeting Basics – Expenses (part 2)

Now we are going to look at some other expenses that may bounce around a bit. We are going to do the same thing as before and pull the last 3 months of bills and determine an average.

$ This section focuses on other expenses such as keeping a car working, keeping ourselves healthy, eating, and other good stuff.

Same as before, the amounts on the following pages are for our example. It is important that you put in **REALISTIC** amounts for where you are today.

Budgeting Basics – Expenses (part 2)

	Yearly Budget	Monthly Budget
EXPENSE		
Car Maintenance	$ 600.00	$ 50.00
Gas	$ 2,400.00	$ 200.00
Life Insurance	$ 1,200.00	$ 100.00
Deductible	$ 900.00	$ 75.00
Prescriptions	$ 300.00	$ 25.00
Groceries	$ 10,200.00	$ 850.00
Kid's Stuff	$ 4,200.00	$ 350.00
Pet Stuff	$ 1,440.00	$ 120.00
Hair	$ 900.00	$ 75.00
Clothing	$ 5,400.00	$ 450.00
Eating out	$ 7,200.00	$ 600.00
Entertainment	$ 6,000.00	$ 500.00

Notes:
$ Items like car maintenance are not spent every month. This money will accumulate until you need new tires or an oil change.
$ Items like your health care deductible will also accumulate so that it is there if you need it.

$ Expenses are starting to add up. It is starting to look like a lot of spending in a year.

$ Let's take a look at more expenses.

The next thing we need to look at is how much debt you need to pay off.

For this example, we are going to assume that we are paying off a balance on 2 credit cards and one home equity loan.

$ You may have more or less consumer debt. If you have more, list out each piece of debt separately.

For our first pass at a budget, put in the minimum you need to pay on your loans/credit cards.

	Yearly Budget	Monthly Budget
EXPENSE		
Debt	$ 1,800.00	$ 150.00
Debt	$ 3,000.00	$ 250.00
Debt	$ 960.00	$ 80.00

$ The above just represent the minimum payments due. At this rate, you will be in debt for many, many years to come.

Let's take a look at one last expense.

Budgeting Basics – Expenses (allowance)

The last thing we need to look at is the most important.

Pay yourself an allowance. It is important to give yourself a little flexibility each month. A good way to avoid an outburst of spending is to allow yourself enough money to have a small indulgence once in awhile. To do this, we build in an allowance each month. This allowance is in cash and can be spent any way you want, so long as you only pay cash. If you want to spend it on fancy lattes, or save up a few months for a bigger purchase, that is up to you.

This should help keep you from thinking you are being deprived.

Budgeting Basics – Expenses (allowance)

	Yearly Budget	**Monthly Budget**
EXPENSE		
Allowance	$ 2,400.00	$ 200.00

$ Remember, this is paid to you in cash each month. You can take it out weekly, bi-monthly (1st and the 15th of the month), or just once a month.

$ It can be spent on whatever you want.

$ Save it or spend it, it is up to you, but always keep this in cash – NO CREDIT CARDS.

$ If you spend a penny over your allowance, you are just stealing from yourself.

Time to put it all together.

Budgeting Basics – TOTAL Expenses

		Yearly Budget		Monthly Budget
%				
INCOME				
Income	$	60,000.00	$	5,000.00
Other Income	$		$	
TOTAL INCOME	**$**	**60,000.00**	**$**	**5,000.00**
EXPENSE				
Mortgage/Rent	$	9,600.00	$	800.00
Utilities	$	2,400.00	$	200.00
Garbage	$	600.00	$	50.00
Cable/Internet	$	1,200.00	$	100.00
Cell Phone	$	1,200.00	$	100.00
Insurance	$	1,200.00	$	100.00
House Maintenance	$	1,200.00	$	100.00
Car Loan	$	5,400.00	$	450.00
Car Insurance	$	1,500.00	$	125.00
Car Maintenance	$	600.00	$	50.00
Gas	$	2,400.00	$	200.00
Life Insurance	$	1,200.00	$	100.00
Deductible	$	900.00	$	75.00
Prescriptions	$	300.00	$	25.00
Groceries	$	10,200.00	$	850.00
Debt	$	1,800.00	$	150.00
Debt	$	3,000.00	$	250.00
Debt	$	960.00	$	80.00
Kid's Stuff	$	4,200.00	$	350.00
Pet Stuff	$	1,440.00	$	120.00
Hair	$	900.00	$	75.00
Clothing	$	5,400.00	$	450.00
Eating Out	$	7,200.00	$	600.00
Entertainment	$	6,000.00	$	500.00
Allowance	$	2,400.00	$	200.00
TOTAL EXPENSES	**$**	**73,200.00**	**$**	**6,100.00**
BALANCE	**$**	**(13,200.00)**	**$**	**(1,100.00)**

Budgeting Basics – TOTAL Expenses

Notes:

$ Over-spending by $1,100 a month equals $13,200 a year of over-spending. This is where consumer debt comes from.

$ If $13,200 is placed on a credit card that accumulated interest at 10% per year, this will cost you approximately $1,500 per year in interest (in addition to paying back the $13,200). Can you say, 'Money Drain!'

OK, we have figured out how much we are spending.

In our example, we are spending $6,100 per month - $73,200 per year.

What is wrong with this picture? – according to our income schedule – we are only earning $5,000 per month.

What does it mean when you have a negative balance?

$ We have a negative balance of $1,100 every month. When this happens, you are spending more than you are making.

$ Then your credit card/consumer debt will increase each month and your minimum payments will continue to rise each month.

$ Remember, accumulating **DEBT** is like trying to drink out of a cup with a hole in the bottom...no fun!

$ If you do not change your behavior, you will be broke and broken.

Looks like it is time to make some changes.

Budgeting Basics
Resetting the budget

Now that you know you are spending more than you earn, what can you do about it?

We will start with the following:

$ Re-examine your income. Let's assume you can work some overtime each month. Take a look at things you can do to increase what you earn each month. **(increase the INS)**

$ Re-examine where you are spending your money. Does it make sense to keep borrowing money to eat out? Working today to pay off stuff you enjoyed months or even years ago is robbing you of future pleasures and robbing you of **Wealthy Living. (decrease the OUTS).**

$ Until your debt is paid off, the lines for Eating Out and Entertaining are gone. Any Eating Out and Entertaining comes out of your **ALLOWANCE**.

Let's see how close that gets us to being in balance.

Budgeting Basics – Positive Balance

%		Yearly Budget		Monthly Budget	
INCOME					
Income	$	66,000.00	$	5,500.00	
Other Income	$		$		
TOTAL INCOME	$	**66,000.00**	$	**5,500.00**	
EXPENSE					
Mortgage/Rent	$	9,600.00	$	800.00	
Utilities	$	2,400.00	$	200.00	
Garbage	$	600.00	$	50.00	
Cable/Internet	$	1,200.00	$	100.00	
Cell Phone	$	1,200.00	$	100.00	
Insurance	$	1,200.00	$	100.00	
House Maintenance	$	1,200.00	$	100.00	
Car Loan	$	5,400.00	$	450.00	
Car Insurance	$	1,500.00	$	125.00	
Car Maintenance	$	600.00	$	50.00	
Gas	$	2,400.00	$	200.00	
Life Insurance	$	1,200.00	$	100.00	
Deductible	$	900.00	$	75.00	
Prescriptions	$	300.00	$	25.00	
Groceries	$	10,200.00	$	850.00	
Debt	$	1,800.00	$	150.00	
Debt	$	3,000.00	$	250.00	
Debt	$	960.00	$	80.00	
Kid's Stuff	$	4,200.00	$	350.00	
Pet Stuff	$	1,440.00	$	120.00	
Hair	$	900.00	$	75.00	
Clothing	$	2,700.00	$	225.00	
Allowance	$	2,400.00	$	200.00	
TOTAL EXPENSES	$	**57,300.00**	$	**4,775.00**	
BALANCE	$	**8,700.00**	$	**725.00**	

Budgeting Basics – Positive Balance

Notes:

$ The lie most people tell themselves before they have a budget is that they don't make enough money. Most people make enough money to have whatever they want, but you have to choose because you don't make enough to have it all at once...nobody does...just ask MC Hammer!

$ You can pay off even more Debt by decreasing the amount of money in the line items below Debt (Kid's Stuff, Pet Stuff, etc.)

$ In this budget we are saving for emergencies, so we'll cover all basic expenses: you can buy clothes, have a little fun, and start paying off that debt...**HURRAH**!

Congratulations, now you have a budget that has a positive balance.

In fact, in our sample budget, we were able to find enough savings to allow an extra $725 per month. Since this is a debt elimination budget, you will put all extra money against your debt to get the balance paid off as soon as possible. When you pay off your first debt, you move onto your next debt.

In our example, after credit card #1 is paid off, we would then payoff credit card #2. After credit card #1 is gone, we will have a total amount of $1,125 to pay off credit card #2. (minimum payment of $250 plus $725 from our positive budget balance plus $150 from the credit card #1 payment which was eliminated).

You can now see how your budget will simultaneously stop the accumulation of debt and actually reverse the process by using the positive budget balance to eliminate your debt!

TIME TO RECONCILE ACTUAL NUMBERS TO BUDGET NUMBERS.........

HOW TO BUILD A FINANCIAL FOUNDATION

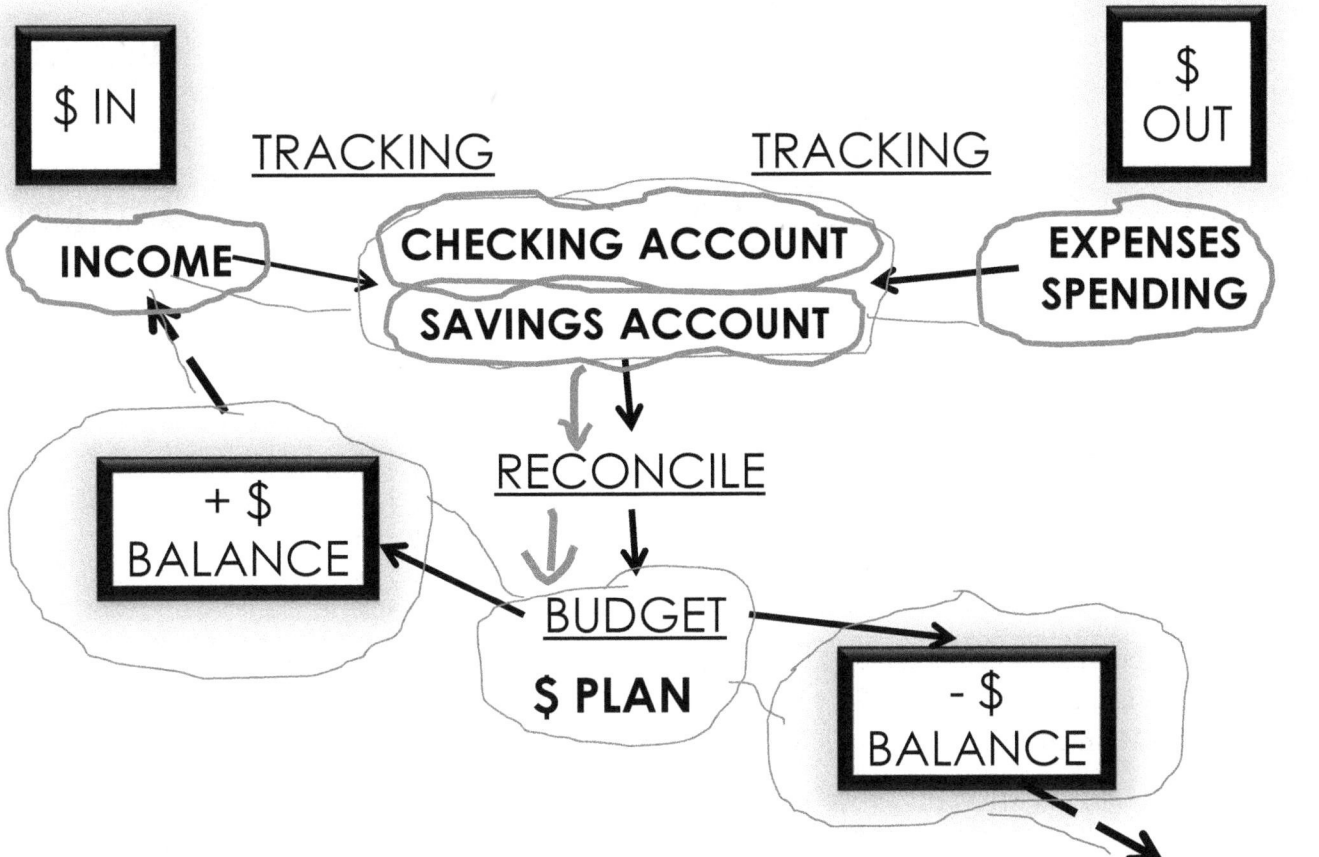

$ IN

$ OUT

TRACKING   TRACKING

INCOME

CHECKING ACCOUNT

SAVINGS ACCOUNT

EXPENSES
SPENDING

+ $
BALANCE

RECONCILE

BUDGET

$ PLAN

- $
BALANCE

DEBT

3 $ KEYS
$ INS
$ OUTS
$ BALANCE

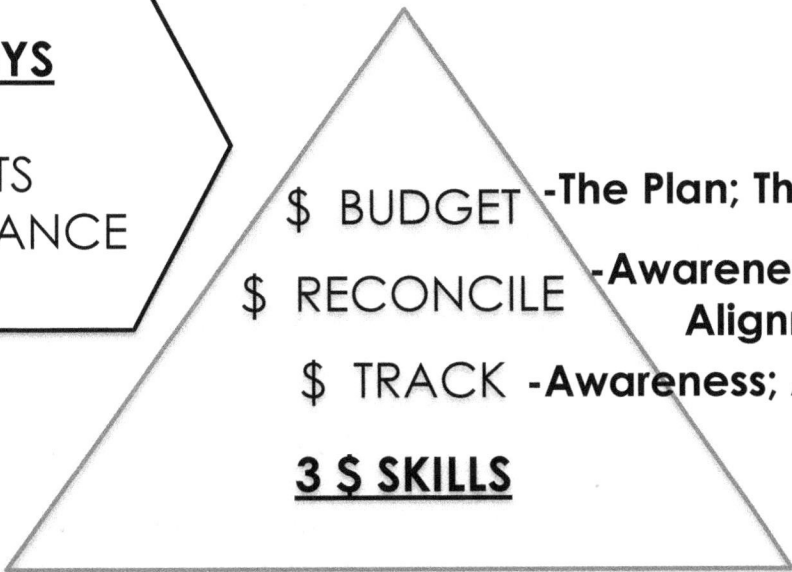

$ BUDGET -The Plan; The How

$ RECONCILE -Awareness; Attention;
Alignment

$ TRACK -Awareness; Attention

3 $ SKILLS

TIME TO RECONCILE ACTUAL NUMBERS TO BUDGET NUMBERS.........

Budgeting Basics – Actual results

%		Yearly Budget		Monthly Budget		Jan Actual		Difference
INCOME								
Income	$	66,000.00	$	5,500.00	$	5,250.00	$	(250.00)
Other Income	$		$		$		$	
TOTAL INCOME	**$**	**66,000.00**	**$**	**5,500.00**	**$**	**5,250.00**	**$**	**(250.00)**
EXPENSE								
Mortgage/Rent	$	9,600.00	$	800.00	$	800.00	$	-
Utilities	$	2,400.00	$	200.00	$	200.00	$	-
Garbage	$	600.00	$	50.00	$	50.00	$	-
Cable/Internet	$	1,200.00	$	100.00	$	100.00	$	-
Cell Phone	$	1,200.00	$	100.00	$	125.00	$	(25.00)
Insurance	$	1,200.00	$	100.00	**$**	**100.00**	$	-
House Maintenance	$	1,200.00	$	100.00	**$**	**100.00**	$	-
Car Loan	$	5,400.00	$	450.00	$	450.00	$	-
Car Insurance	$	1,500.00	$	125.00	**$**	**125.00**	$	-
Car Maintenance	$	600.00	$	50.00	**$**	**50.00**	$	-
Gas	$	2,400.00	$	200.00	$	225.00	$	(25.00)
Life Insurance	$	1,200.00	$	100.00	**$**	**100.00**	$	-
Deductible	$	900.00	$	75.00	**$**	**75.00**	$	-
Prescriptions	$	300.00	$	25.00	$	25.00	$	-
Groceries	$	10,200.00	$	850.00	$	900.00	$	(50.00)
Debt	$	10,500.00	$	875.00	$	530.00	$	345.00
Debt	$	3,000.00	$	250.00	$	250.00	$	-
Debt	$	960.00	$	80.00	$	80.00	$	-
Kid's Stuff	$	4,200.00	$	350.00	$	300.00	$	50.00
Pet Stuff	$	1,440.00	$	120.00	$	100.00	$	20.00
Hair	$	900.00	$	75.00	$	90.00	$	(15.00)
Clothing	$	2,700.00	$	225.00	$	275.00	$	(50.00)
Allowance	$	2,400.00	$	200.00	$	200.00	$	-
TOTAL EXPENSES	**$**	**66,000.00**	**$**	**5,500.00**	**$**	**5,250.00**	**$**	**250.00**
BALANCE	$	-	$	-	$	-	$	-

Highlight:

$ We saved $250 (The **BOLD** numbers in Jan Actual Column) this month for emergencies, long term maintenance, and future bills (like insurance). This money can accumulate in your checking account or can be transferred to savings. Don't look at your account balance and think, "Shopping Spree!" No, no, no!

$ We didn't hit our budgeted payment of $875 for our debt, but we did pay an extra $380 on our debt. (Minimum payment of $150 less actual payment of $530) HURRAH!

$ We did not accumulate any new debt. Double HURRAH!!

Budgeting Basics – Actual results

So what happened? Let's review how we did in the first month with our sample budget:

$ Our **Income** came in a bit lower than we expected. First, re-examine the options to increase income. We may need to reset the budget if our expectation is unreasonable.

$ Examine our **Expenses/Spending** – how did we do? We came in lower in some areas and over in others. We seem to still be struggling to keep our spending down on clothing, and our grocery bill was high. Re-examine how we can save in these areas. Discipline takes some time so don't give up, think about what you are spending your money on.

$ On a positive note, we did all our eating out and entertaining from our allowance, and because we did, we have money to apply to our debt.

Keep up the good work.

The effect of the **INS** and **OUTS** is that there was less money paid against debt from credit card #1 than we wanted. However, we are moving in the right direction. Keep working on increasing income, reducing expenses, and putting extra money against debt balances.

Budgeting Basics – WEALTHY LIVING

This is the **WEALTHY LIVING** habit

Each month:

$ Fill in your actual **Income** and **Expenses** at least weekly or as you pay your bills.

$ At the end of each month, compare your budget to your actuals. Do you have money left over? Did you overspend?

$ Remember, your results are not an accident or something that was done to you. If you followed your positive balance budget, you will have money at the end of the month to pay off your debt. If you overspend, you stole not only money but also part of your future from yourself.

$ What do I mean you stole from your future? Remember, some of your money in your budget is being set aside for the bills that don't come each month – insurance, car repairs. You will have to make that amount up next month. Do you see how the debt accumulates?

$ Remember, if you have debt, you didn't accumulate it in a month and you won't make it go away in a month...

...you will have to practice, practice, practice!

Consumer Debt Elimination Budget

%		Yearly Budget	Monthly Budget	Jan Actual	Difference
	INCOME				
	Income	$	$	$	$
	Other Income	$	$	$	$
	TOTAL INCOME	$	$	$	$
	EXPENSE				
	Mortgage/Rent	$	$	$	$
	Utilities	$	$	$	$
	Garbage	$	$	$	$
	Cable/Internet	$	$	$	$
	Cell Phone	$	$	$	$
	Insurance	$	$		
	House Maintenance	$	$	$	$
	Car Loan	$	$	$	$
	Car Insurance	$	$	$	$
	Car Maintenance	$	$	$	$
	Gas	$	$	$	$
	Life Insurance	$	$	$	$
	Deductible	$	$	$	$
	Prescriptions	$	$	$	$
	Groceries	$	$	$	$
	Debt	$	$	$	$
	Debt	$	$	$	$
	Debt	$	$	$	$
	Kid's Stuff	$	$	$	$
	Pet Stuff	$	$	$	$
	Hair	$	$	$	$
	Clothing	$	$	$	$
	Allowance	$	$	$	$
	TOTAL EXPENSES	$	$	$	$
	BALANCE	$	$	$	$

Consumer Debt Elimination
Budget Highlights

$ First, there are three areas of your budget that you can control: The **INS**, The **OUTS**, and the **BALANCE**.

$ Get your **income** up, up, up. Get your **expenses** down, down, down. And make sure your **BALANCE** is positive, positive, positive.

$ Your goal with this budget is to **KILL YOUR DEBT!**

$ **Every extra penny goes to paying off debt! Check out "Debt Pay-Off Schedule ~ Seeing How Every Penny Counts" (pages 188-193).**

$ In this phase of budgeting, the slogan is: 'If you can't eat it, you don't need it!'

$ In this phase you are boiling life down to the simplest necessities.

$ It is like a restart on your financial life.

$ The goal here is focus, focus, focus.

$ This can be frustrating. Other items will 'pop' up. You will have to face the mess that you have created. Please remember that you did not create this mess overnight. It will take some time to create new habits and learn new skills. Be patient with yourself.

$ Time is your friend.

$ Have fun, be creative, and challenge old beliefs and behaviors.

Remember: If you cheat, you are only cheating yourself!

Short Term Savings Budget

	Yearly Budget	Monthly Budget	Jan Actual	Difference
%				
INCOME				
Income	$	$	$	$
Other Income	$	$	$	$
S/T Savings	$	$	$	$
TOTAL INCOME	$	$	$	$
EXPENSE				
Mortgage/Rent	$	$	$	$
Utilities	$	$	$	$
Garbage	$	$	$	$
Cable/Internet	$	$	$	$
Cell Phone	$	$	$	$
Insurance	$	$	$	$
House Maintenance	$	$	$	$
Car Loan	$	$	$	$
Car Insurance	$	$	$	$
Car Maintenance	$	$	$	$
Gas	$	$	$	$
Life Insurance	$	$	$	$
Deductible	$	$	$	$
Prescriptions	$	$	$	$
Groceries	$	$	$	$
Kid's Stuff	$	$	$	$
Pet Stuff	$	$	$	$
Hair	$	$	$	$
Clothing	$	$	$	$
Allowance	$	$	$	$
TOTAL EXPENSES	$	$	$	$
BALANCE	$	$	$	$

Short Term Savings Budget

Notes:

$ Debt is gone except for the Car Loan and Mortgage. Work on getting rid of the Car Loan.

$ All 'extra' money is placed in S/T Savings (S/T = Short Term). This is your Emergency Fund.

$ Keep 3 – 9 months of your total expenses in your emergency fund.

$ Note that S/T Savings comes out of the Net Income number. Your available income less your S/T Savings = the money you have available for your expenses/spending. You are now learning the **HABIT** of paying yourself first. You are investing in yourself, your values, your future, and your plans!

$ Stay **FOCUSED** each month.

Short Term Savings Budget

%		Yearly Budget	Monthly Budget	Jan Actual	Difference
	INCOME				
	Income	$	$	$	$
	Other Income	$	$	$	$
	S/T Savings	$	$	$	$
	TOTAL INCOME	$	$	$	$
	EXPENSE				
	Mortgage/Rent	$	$	$	$
	Utilities	$	$	$	$
	Garbage	$	$	$	$
	Cable/Internet	$	$	$	$
	Cell Phone	$	$	$	$
	Insurance	$	$	$	$
	House Maintenance	$	$	$	$
	Car Loan	$	$	$	$
	Car Insurance	$	$	$	$
	Car Maintenance	$	$	$	$
	Gas	$	$	$	$
	Life Insurance	$	$	$	$
	Deductible	$	$	$	$
	Prescriptions	$	$	$	$
	Groceries	$	$	$	$
	Kid's Stuff	$	$	$	$
	Pet Stuff	$	$	$	$
	Hair	$	$	$	$
	Clothing	$	$	$	$
	Allowance	$	$	$	$
	TOTAL EXPENSES	$	$	$	$
	BALANCE	$	$	$	$

Short Term Savings Budget

If you have no consumer debt, then this is the **BUDGET** for you:

$ The process is the same as described in the debt elimination section pages 55 - 79. Your budget will balance to zero. All extra money goes to fund your **Short Term Savings**.

$ Since you have no consumer debt to pay off, you will now begin to accumulate **Short Term Savings**.

$ **Short Term Savings** is also called an emergency fund.

$ This is money set aside for those 'Stuff Happens', 'OOPS', unexpected moments and events. We all have them.

$ Your **Short Term Savings** should be 3 – 9 months of your monthly income. How do you decide? You need to think about questions like: How easily can I replace my current income? How much stability do I want to provide for my family in a tough situation? How far back can we cut our expenses?

$ Once you have established an amount for yourself, all the positive balance from your monthly budget is deposited into a savings account.

This money is not for vacation, new furniture, parties or other 'I want' items. It sits and is there for you as stability in your financial foundation.

Long Term Savings Budget

		Yearly	Monthly	Jan	
%		Budget	Budget	Actual	Difference
INCOME					
Income		$	$	$	$
Other Income		$	$	$	$
L/T Savings		$	$	$	$
TOTAL INCOME		$	$	$	$
EXPENSE					
Mortgage/Rent		$	$	$	$
Utilities		$	$	$	$
Garbage		$	$	$	$
Cable/Internet		$	$	$	$
Cell Phone		$	$	$	$
Insurance		$	$	$	$
House Maintenance		$	$	$	$
Car Insurance		$	$	$	$
Car Maintenance		$	$	$	$
Gas		$	$	$	$
Life Insurance		$	$	$	$
Prescriptions		$	$	$	$
Groceries		$	$	$	$
Kid's Stuff		$	$	$	$
Pet Stuff		$	$	$	$
Hair		$	$	$	$
Clothing		$	$	$	$
Allowance		$	$	$	$
TOTAL EXPENSES		$	$	$	$
BALANCE		$	$	$	$

Long Term Savings Budget

Notes:

$ Your emergency fund is established.

$ There is no more Car Loan, EVER.

$ You are now working on your L/T Savings (L/T = Long Term). This is your retirement and/or your children's education.

$ At this point you may decide to pay off your Mortgage. On one hand this is a very stable investment where you can calculate the rate of return. On the other hand, you cannot eat your home, meaning the money is not easily available to you if needed. You will have to choose.

$ At this point you may want to add a line in your budget titled 'Special' which could be for items such as a vacation, furniture, or some other special purchase.

$ The 'Special' line is not included here because it really depends on your age and how far behind you are on saving for retirement and education.

$ Notice the allowance line is still in place. Respect it! Don't steal from yourself!!

Long Term Savings Budget

		Yearly	Monthly	Jan	
%		Budget	Budget	Actual	Difference
INCOME					
Income		$	$	$	$
Other Income		$	$	$	$
L/T Savings		$	$	$	$
TOTAL INCOME		$	$	$	$
EXPENSE					
Mortgage/Rent		$	$	$	$
Utilities		$	$	$	$
Garbage		$	$	$	$
Cable/Internet		$	$	$	$
Cell Phone		$	$	$	$
Insurance		$	$	$	$
House Maintenance		$	$	$	$
Car Insurance		$	$	$	$
Car Maintenance		$	$	$	$
Gas		$	$	$	$
Life Insurance		$	$	$	$
Prescriptions		$	$	$	$
Groceries		$	$	$	$
Kid's Stuff		$	$	$	$
Pet Stuff		$	$	$	$
Hair		$	$	$	$
Clothing		$	$	$	$
Allowance		$	$	$	$
TOTAL EXPENSES		$	$	$	$
BALANCE		$	$	$	$

Long Term Savings Budget

If you have no consumer debt and have short term savings, then this is the **BUDGET** for you.

CONGRATULATIONS! This is where things get really fun!

$ OK, notice where your **Long Term Savings** is located on the budget. It is above expenses in the Income section.

$ **You are going to pay yourself first.**

$ This money is going to create income for you for your future.

$ **Long Term Savings** is 15% – 20% of your income. (Or more!)

$ **Long Term Savings** is for retirement and education.

$ Have it taken straight out of your income and budget on what remains (net income less **Long Term Savings**)

$ If you have a positive balance after saving 15% – 20%, then you get to decide what the positive balance is used for: Pay the house off? Save for a special vacation? Save for new furniture? Save for a new car? Put more into retirement?

At this point, the choice is yours!

Passive Income/Earned Income Budget

%		Yearly Budget	Monthly Budget	Jan Actual	Difference
	INCOME				
	Passive Income	$	$	$	$
	Income	$	$	$	$
	L/T Savings	$	$	$	$
	TOTAL INCOME	$	$	$	$
	EXPENSE				
	Mortgage/Rent	$	$	$	$
	Utilities	$	$	$	$
	Garbage	$	$	$	$
	Cable/Internet	$	$	$	$
	Cell Phone	$	$	$	$
	Insurance	$	$	$	$
	House Maintenance	$	$	$	$
	Car Insurance	$	$	$	$
	Car Maintenance	$	$	$	$
	Gas	$	$	$	$
	Life Insurance	$	$	$	$
	Prescriptions	$	$	$	$
	Groceries	$	$	$	$
	Special	$	$	$	$
	Kid's Stuff	$	$	$	$
	Pet Stuff	$	$	$	$
	Hair	$	$	$	$
	Clothing	$	$	$	$
	Allowance	$	$	$	$
	TOTAL EXPENSES	$	$	$	$
	BALANCE	$	$	$	$

Passive Income/Earned Income Budget

Notes:

$ AHHH! This is the GOLD standard.

$ Passive Income is when your money, investments, and projects are working for you. Your money is generating its own income not based on your actual daily activity.

$ Think retirement!

$ Your Mortgage may or may not be paid off. This is a personal choice that will have to be looked at in detail.

$ You are still Saving - paying yourself first.

$ You may choose to work or may need to work. You do not want to outlive your money.

$ You still have an allowance.

$ This is definitely the time to have a 'Special' line in your budget.

$ You are still **BUDGETING!**

Passive Income/Earned Income Budget

%		Yearly Budget	Monthly Budget	Jan Actual	Difference
	INCOME				
	Passive Income	$	$	$	$
	Income	$	$	$	$
	L/T Savings	$	$	$	$
	TOTAL INCOME	$	$	$	$
	EXPENSE				
	Mortgage/Rent	$	$	$	$
	Utilities	$	$	$	$
	Garbage	$	$	$	$
	Cable/Internet	$	$	$	$
	Cell Phone	$	$	$	$
	Insurance	$	$	$	$
	House Maintenance	$	$	$	$
	Car Insurance	$	$	$	$
	Car Maintenance	$	$	$	$
	Gas	$	$	$	$
	Life Insurance	$	$	$	$
	Prescriptions	$	$	$	$
	Groceries	$	$	$	$
	Special	$	$	$	$
	Kid's Stuff	$	$	$	$
	Pet Stuff	$	$	$	$
	Hair	$	$	$	$
	Clothing	$	$	$	$
	Allowance	$	$	$	$
	TOTAL EXPENSES	$	$	$	$
	BALANCE	$	$	$	$

Passive Income/Earned Income Budget

This is the ultimate goal!

The income you receive from your investment of your Long Term Savings replaces your income.

So let's say from our budgeting we would like to have $100,000 a year as our **INS**:

If you have approximately $1,500,000 in Long Term Savings earning an average of 10% per year, then you would earn approximately $150,000 per year on your money. Uncle Sam will take approximately 35% ($52,500) which would leave you with approximately $100,000 for your **INS** budget.

Please notice: you are still budgeting, you are still saving, and you are still applying all the **HABITS** of **WEALTHY LIVING**. It never ends – there is no destination, only a journey that lasts a lifetime.

Develop Your Skills

Two additional tools are included in Appendix 3 & Appendix 4.

These are two very important skills for you to master.

$ A Statement of Net Worth (Appendix 3, p. 184-185). This is also known as a Personal Financial Statement. This form gives you a snapshot on a specific date of the total value of everything you own less everything you owe. It is a very useful tool for tracking your progress.

$ The Time Value of Money (Appendix 4, p. 186-187). When you invest your money, it grows over time. When you have debt, this same concept eats your money and your future. This concept is like gravity; it just is, and it applies to everybody in the same way. There are great opportunities in this concept!

Whether you think you can
or
you think you can't,
you're right!

~ Henry Ford

$\$^+$

DEVELOP YOUR SKILLS

FOUR STEPS TO WEALTHY LIVING

Step 3:

CLARIFY YOUR VALUES

~ VALUES ~

RELATIVE

WORTH or IMPORTANCE

$\$^+$

CLARIFY
YOUR
VALUES

Clarify Your Values

Question: Shouldn't I do this section before the Develop Your Skills section?

Answer: NO! Developing Your Skills is a key foundation step and must be in place before you begin to Clarify Your Values. There is no point in marching off to create a certain type of life if you have a mess to clean up. And when you are creating your desired life, you must have the appropriate skills in place to maintain it.

REMEMBER:

Building a Wealthy Life
is like building a house…
you have to
start with a good foundation.

Clarify Your Values

Defining Wealth

There are two components.

Component One:

Your money as it is right now which you identified through **Developing Your Skills:**

$ First Goal: Pay off Debt

$ Second Goal: Have an Emergency Fund

$ Third Goal: Pay Yourself First

Component Two:

Clarify your Values:

$ Know what you **Value**

$ Boil what you **Value** down to the essence

$ Turn wants into **Values**

$ Open yourself up to discovering, finding, and experiencing what you **Value** right now with what you have

Clarify Your Values

The first component of defining **Wealth** is tangible.
It is simple math,
and you use the **SKILLS** in section two to obtain it.

Developing your Skills
$ First Goal: Pay off Debt
$ Second Goal: Have an Emergency Fund
$ Third Goal: Pay Yourself First

As you pay off debt, you free up money to continue the process. Once you pay off all of your debt (and accumulate no more ever), you have now FREED yourself. Freedom is of Value. To be free is to have Wealth.

Next, you establish and maintain an emergency fund.   An emergency fund provides stability. Stability can be defined as 'the strength to endure' or 'resistance to outside conditions or disturbance'. Creating financial stability is key to a strong foundation.   When 'stuff happens' (and 'stuff' always happens), you have the resources to respond without disturbing what you have created. To have stability is to have Wealth.

Paying yourself first creates the resources to fund the rest of your life. At this point, you are now ready to start defining what it is that you value and what you will create with your money and your life...

Clarify Your Values

The second component of defining **Wealth** is to **Clarify your Values**. This is individualized.

Too often in our culture, we get caught up in the 'Hollywood' version of being **Wealthy**. We see it on TV or at the movies, and we start to believe that if we don't have the car, the house, or the fashion, we are not Wealthy. In addition, when we see it on TV, it appears to be instant. We can look at what other people have and not appreciate what it took for them to achieve it. Then we begin to believe that that type of wealth is out of our reach. If we attempt to create the 'Hollywood' version of Wealth for ourselves, we create debt. We chase and chase and chase and we are never happy. We pine for what we do not have instead of appreciating and enjoying what we do have. Why?

Because this is not an individualized expression of **Wealthy Living.**

Let's do an experiment together to demonstrate this idea of Individualized Expression.

Experiment Time

Instructions: I am going to give you a word on the next page. First, let a picture of the word come to your mind. Then on that page, write down descriptive words that describe the word.

Go to the next page when you are ready to begin...

DOG

$+

CLARIFY YOUR VALUES

Individualized Expression

Now, Each person's idea or picture or description of a 'DOG' is going to be a little different. Some will be big dogs, some will be small dogs, with long hair, short hair, a variety of colors, long noses, short noses, pointy ears, floppy ears, big barks, soft barks, drooly, licky, playful, athletic, snuggly... None are right and none are wrong. Each is an individualized expression of 'DOG', but each is a 'DOG'. (except for those of you who wrote 'CAT', and I know there are a few. Yours is still an individualized expression and good for you for following your gut!)

Defining Wealth Works the Same Way

If one person's idea of being **Wealthy** is having a beautiful garden and another's is eating a beautifully prepared lunch and another's is having a coffee pot that turns on before getting out of bed and another's is a sail boat, that's okay. None is right and none is wrong. None is good and none is bad.

Each is an individualized expression. It is all good provided it is in alignment with what **YOU** **VALUE**.

103

Clarify Your Values

So how do you Clarify Your Values?

The answer must come from the inside out.

On page 107, there is a question. On the blank page provided (on page 106) write down everything that comes to your mind. Be specific and have fun with it. Really sit and think about it.

Remember: NO LIMITS

Happiness is that state
of consciousness
which proceeds from
the achievement
of one's values.

~ Ayn Rand

$+

CLARIFY
YOUR
VALUES

YOUR LIST

You have unlimited resources.

What would you buy?
What would you experience?
Where would you go?
Who would you take with you?

$⁺

CLARIFY
YOUR
VALUES

That was fun!

Now take your list from page 106 and look it over...

$ If you only had a **year** to live, what would you eliminate?

$ Cross out what you would eliminate on page 106.

$ On page 109 write what remains.

$ If you would like to add something, do so.

**When you are ready,
follow the instructions on page 110...**

YOUR LIST (ONE YEAR)

Next Step

Now take a look at your list from page 109...

$ If you only had a **month** to live, what would you eliminate?

$ Cross out what you would eliminate on page 109.

$ On page 111 write what remains.

$ If you would like to add something, do so.

When you are ready, go to page 112...

YOUR LIST (ONE MONTH)

One more time

Now take a look at your list from page 111...

$ If you only had **24 hours** to live, what would you eliminate?

$ Cross out what you would eliminate on page 111.

$ On page 113 write what remains.

$ If you would like to add something, do so.

What is still on the page is what YOU VALUE.

YOUR LIST (24 HOURS)

What is still on the page is what YOU VALUE

What might surprise you is that what you have listed on page 113 may be very similar to what you wrote down on page 19 (the 'This is Wealthy Living' worksheet). Take some time to compare page 19 to your Values list from this exercise. Adjust your Values list if necessary.

On the next page is another 'This is Wealthy Living' worksheet. Go ahead and write down what YOU VALUE.

THIS IS WEALTHY LIVING

THIS IS YOU AND YOU ARE THIS

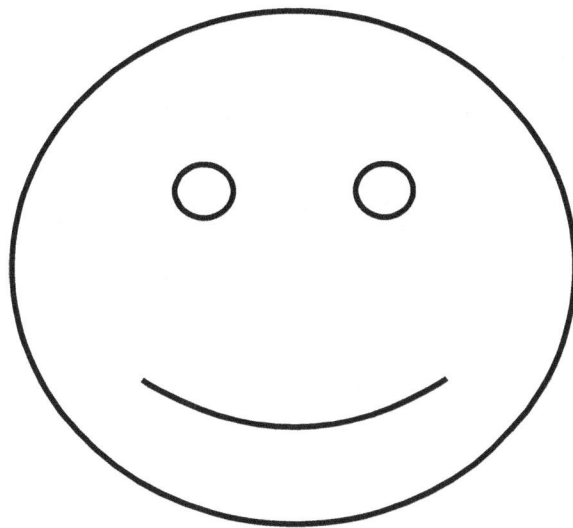

YOUR VALUES

ESSENCE

The most significant element, quality or aspect of a thing or person.

$\$^{+}$

CLARIFY YOUR VALUES

Clarify Your Values

~ ESSENCE ~

'The most significant element,
quality or aspect of a thing or person'

Getting to the **ESSENCE** of what you **VALUE** will simplify all areas of your financial life and keep you on track towards Wealthy Living.

To get to the **ESSENCE** of what you **VALUE**, you must let go of the attachments of how it 'should' look or how you have always done something.

This is where creativity, playfulness, and a 'Child-Like' attitude will be very beneficial.

Getting to the **ESSENCE** of what you **VALUE** allows you to have whatever you desire now in the present moment with the resources you currently have.

The ESSENCE of Your VALUES

~ An Example of ESSENCE ~

A family of five places a high **VALUE** on having a peaceful house and family time. Mom and Dad are both tired by the end of the week, and neither wants to cook. They order pizza at a cost of $40 on Friday nights and have family pizza night. This is within the family budget, and everyone's happy. Then one day Mom and Dad look at the budget and realize that Friday, family pizza night, will cost them almost $2,000 a year. Seems like a lot for pizza. They question whether that is really how they want to spend that much money or not. They ask, 'what is it that we really want?' The **ESSENCE**: neither wants to cook and clean up the kitchen on Friday nights, but they both want the family to be together to share a meal and start the weekend in a relaxing way. Mom and Dad agree to be open to finding a more inexpensive way to create the same results. The next day Mom finds a solution. Shopping at a local store, she comes across a box of three frozen pizzas for $13. That is a weekly savings of $27 or approximately $1,300 less a year. **Ah, ESSENCE!** If you know what you value and boil it down to its **ESSENCE** (the most significant element, quality, or aspect), you can then open yourself up to discovering, finding, and experiencing what you **VALUE** right now.

The ESSENCE of Your VALUES

Sometimes getting to the **ESSENCE** of what you **VALUE** is really about looking at what you want. 'Wants' are the activities, places, people, or things that you are drawn to. However these activities, places, people, or things do not always fit into our current circumstances or budgets. Taking a good look at your wants and understanding why you have a strong attraction to that activity, place, person, or thing will lead you to a **VALUE** which can be boiled down to the **ESSENCE** of that **VALUE**. You can then open yourself up to discovering, finding, and experiencing the **ESSENCE** of that want right now.

Let's say you really want to have a massage every week. However, a weekly massage is just not in your budget. Now, if you focus on what you lack, that attracts more of what you don't want (lack), and it could lead to habits that do not support **WEALTHY LIVING** (like going to get the massages anyway and accumulating debt).

The following page will walk you through questions to ask yourself. These will help you take your wants and boil them down to the **ESSENCE** of what you **VALUE**.

The ESSENCE of Your VALUES

EXAMPLE: WEEKLY MASSAGE

$ **I really want** <u>a weekly massage</u>.

$ **I want** <u>a weekly massage</u> **because I VALUE** <u>self-care, but I feel like I am not getting any. This would give it to me</u>. (Big 'Ah-ha!' here)

$ **What does** <u>self-care</u> **mean to me**? <u>Time by myself, doing things I love just for me</u>…

$ **What are some other ways within my budget to demonstrate these qualities right now**? <u>I could schedule a weekly date with myself to read, take a bath with candles and music, hike in my favorite park, etc.</u>

Questions for turning wants into VALUES:

$ I really want_____

$ I want _____ because I **VALUE**

_____

$ What does _____

mean to me? (make a list of the qualities)

_____

$ What are some other ways within my budget to demonstrate these qualities right now? (make a list)

_____

The ESSENCE of Your VALUES

Turning wants into VALUES:

$ I really want_____

$ I want _____ because I **VALUE**

_____

$ What   does   _____

mean to me? (make a list of the qualities)

_____

$ What are some other ways within my budget to demonstrate these qualities right now? (make a list)

_____

Turning wants into VALUES:

$ I really want_____

$ I want _____ because I **VALUE**

_____

$ What   does   _____

mean to me? (make a list of the qualities of)

_____

$ What are some other ways within my budget to demonstrate these qualities right now? (make a list)

_____

Wealthy Living is an Individualized Expression of what YOU VALUE.

$+

CLARIFY YOUR VALUES

Clarify Your Values

Story Time

The kids' spring break was coming up. The husband's work became very busy around that time of year, so he could not get away. Jokingly the wife said to him, 'I should take the kids and go to the beach in California'. The wife was originally from there and had wanted to go back and take the kids. He didn't even hesitate, 'You should do that!' As the wife began to think about the trip, she thought that she would really like to bring another adult with her to help with the kids. Her mother instantly came to mind. A few weeks later, her husband asked if she had booked the tickets and made plans. She said no, she hadn't. He asked, 'Why not?'. She stated that because of all the people she knows that aren't saving any money that she was freaked out about spending the money. 'What if we don't have enough when we are older?' she asked. He asked her in return, 'What are you going to think when we have millions of dollars in our investments and you didn't take this trip?' She booked the trip the next day. She realized that if she had 24 hours to live, she would spend that time with the people she loved on a beach in California. The trip cost about $5,000, and it was worth every penny to be able to take her kids to her high school and the house she grew up in, as well as to hang out on the beach with them and her mom.

(Disclaimer: she had no debt other than their home, and paid cash for the entire trip. This cash did not come out of their emergency fund or any other fund. This was money available to spend on what they Value.)

FOUR STEPS
TO
WEALTHY LIVING

Step 4:

HONOR YOUR INTEGRITY

Go confidently in the direction of your dreams. Live the life you have imagined.

~ Thoreau~

$\$^{+}$

HONOR YOUR INTEGRITY

Honor Your Integrity

'Honor your INTEGRITY' means...

What you **BELIEVE** is in complete alignment with what you **VALUE**. Your **PLAN** for your money is in complete alignment with what you **VALUE**. Your **GOALS**, **FOCUS**, and **COMMITMENT** are in complete alignment with what you **VALUE**. Finally, your <u>daily</u> **BEHAVIORS**, **ACTIONS**, and **DECISIONS** are in complete alignment with what you **VALUE**.

Honor Your Integrity

This fourth step is the glue
that holds it all together.

Without this final step, you will not be successful with your money and will fail to live a **Wealthy Life**.

Here is what unsuccessful people do:

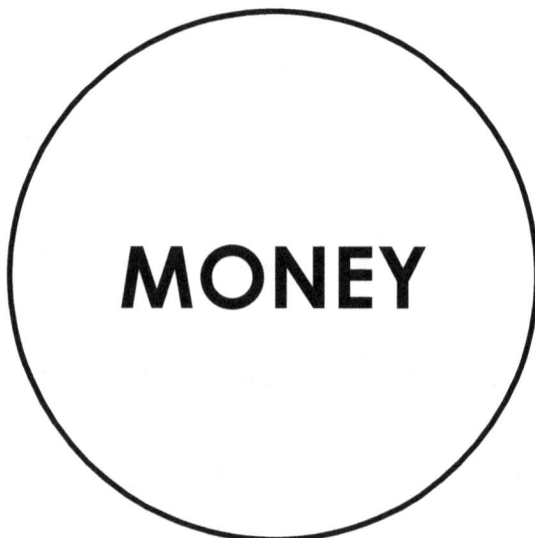

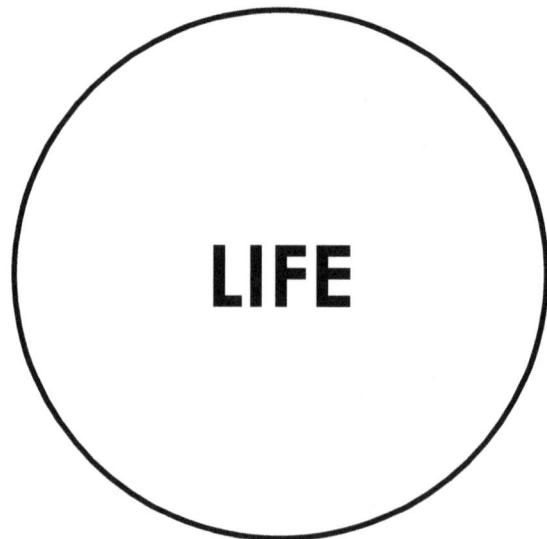

MONEY   **LIFE**

They keep their money
and their life separate

Honor Your Integrity

This fourth step is the glue
that holds it all together.

So, even if you have:

$ Explored your BELIEFS about money and wealth,
$ Developed your SKILLS about money and wealth, and
$ Clarified your VALUES,

If you don't:

≠ Honor your INTEGRITY around your money and your wealth,

Then:

∅ Your everyday behaviors, actions, and decisions will not reflect what you value. A disconnect between what you truly value and how you behave will not lead you to being successful with your money and living a Wealthy Life.

Honor Your Integrity

Here is what
HONORING YOUR INTEGRITY
looks like:

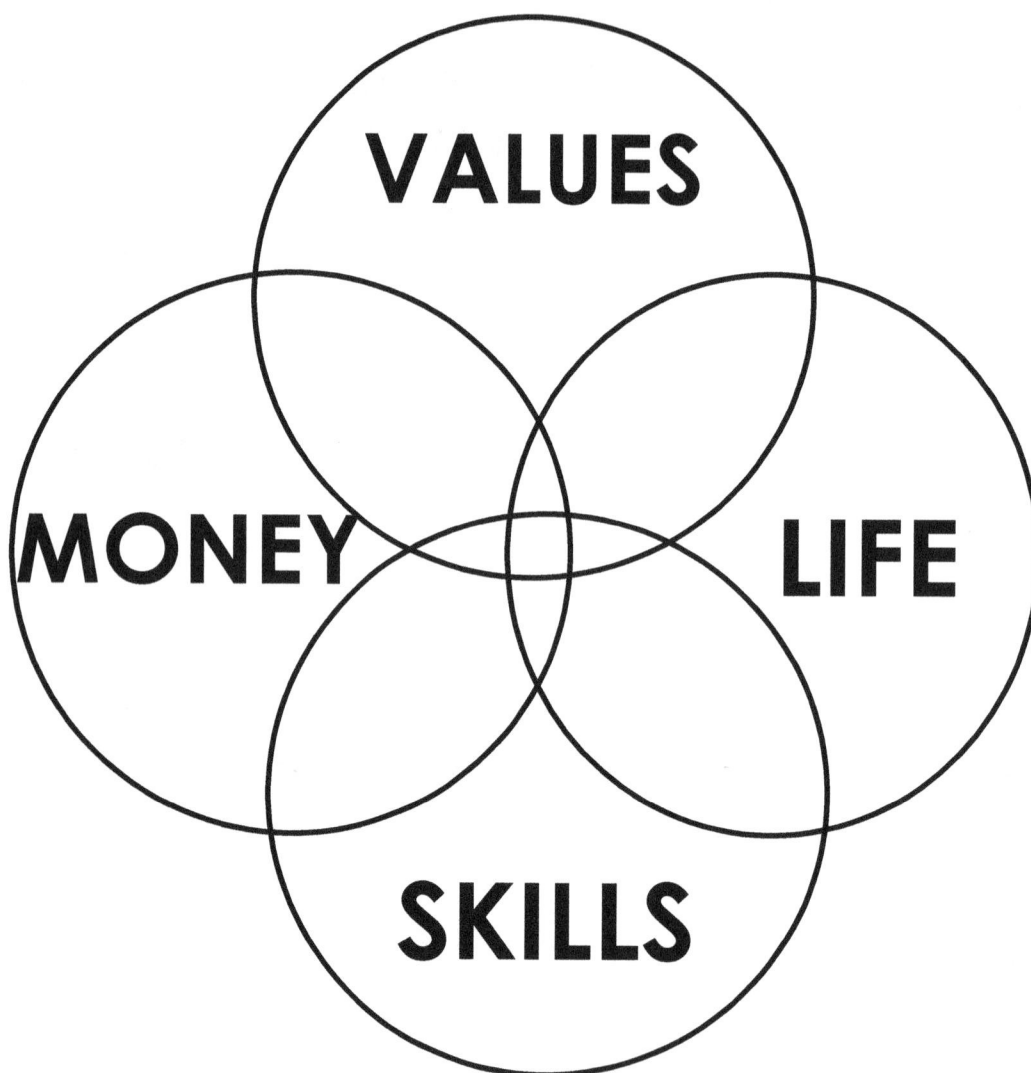

VALUES

MONEY

LIFE

SKILLS

Honor Your Integrity

Integrity:

'Quality or state of being complete or undivided'

Honor Your Integrity

'Honor your INTEGRITY' means...

What you **BELIEVE** is in complete alignment with what you **VALUE**. Your **PLAN** for your money is in complete alignment with what you **VALUE**. Your **GOALS**, **FOCUS**, and **COMMITMENT** are in complete alignment with what you **VALUE**. Finally, your <u>daily</u> **BEHAVIORS**, **ACTIONS**, and **DECISIONS** are in complete alignment with what you **VALUE**.

Building a Wealthy Life is like building a house….

You have to start with a good foundation.

$+

HONOR YOUR INTEGRITY

Honor Your Integrity

So, lets talk about a
ROCK SOLID FINANCIAL FOUNDATION.

$ You start with your **VALUES**. **EXAMPLE:** I **VALUE** creating a financially fantastic life.

$ Check in with yourself: 'Are my **BELIEFS** in alignment with my **VALUES**?' **EXAMPLE:** 'I **VALUE** creating a financially fantastic life' becomes 'I **BELIEVE** I am able to pay off my debt.'

$ Make sure your **BELIEFS** and **BEHAVIOR** are in alignment. **EXAMPLE:** 'I **BELIEVE** I am able to pay off my debt' becomes my **BEHAVIOR**: 'All extra money goes toward debt reduction.' **Question** - 'Hey, want to go out to dinner tonight?' **Answer** – 'I am paying off my debt but I would love to hang out! Come over and we can watch a movie.'

$ You have **DEVELOPED YOUR SKILLS** and you have a **BUDGET**. You **TRACK** your money and **RECONCILE** to your **BUDGET** how you are spending your money. **EXAMPLE:** Using your **SKILLS** – you have a BUDGET– turns into **HONORING YOUR INTEGRITY:** you stick to the **BUDGET** and you **TRACK** your money daily. Every month, you **RECONCILE** how you spend your money to your **BUDGET**.

$ All your **FOCUS, PLANS, GOALS, DECISIONS,** and **ACTIONS** come back to your **VALUES**. This is **HONORING YOUR INTEGRITY**.

IT IS THAT SIMPLE!

Honor Your Integrity

INTEGRITY

| DECISIONS | ACTIONS |

| FOCUS | PLANS | GOALS |

| BELIEFS | BEHAVIOR | SKILLS | BUDGET |

VALUES

$$$ ~ A ROCK SOLID FOUNDATION! ~ $$$

Honor Your Integrity

EXAMPLES OF HONORING YOUR INTEGRITY

The starting point is knowing what you VALUE. Let's say you VALUE stability. For you, you want to be able to stay calm and have your life flow as regularly as possible, even if a 'life problem' shows up. The best way to do that financially would be to have a healthy emergency fund and the proper insurance. But let's say that you don't have any emergency fund or renter's insurance (we are assuming you are a renter). However, you get your nails done once a week, you go out to eat with friends on Friday and sometimes Saturday night, and you get yourself a $4 coffee several times a week. This behavior is **<u>NOT</u> HONORING YOUR INTEGRITY**. Your behavior says 'I live for the moment', but what YOU really value is stability. If your apartment is broken into and your TV, stereo, furniture, and kitchen items are stolen, you will have to replace all of it. But you don't have renter's insurance or an emergency fund. Suppose your car needs new tires and your cat needs to go to the vet. You have not budgeted for these things and you have no emergency fund. You can see how fast things can go downhill when you don't **HONOR YOUR INTEGRITY**. However, if you take the money spent on manicures, coffee, and eating out, using it to build an emergency fund and to purchase renter's insurance before anything else, you would be **HONORING YOUR INTEGRITY**.

Honor Your Integrity

Let's do some more exploring of this idea of **HONORING YOUR INTEGRITY**.

$ So you want to get your income up by earning a promotion at work. How would you go about HONORING earning a promotion? By showing up on time (or even a little early), doing great work, bringing new ideas, and having a great attitude.

$ So you want a new car. How would you go about HONORING saving for a new car? By sticking to your budget, choosing not to eat out, deciding not to buy new items except when old ones wear out, and earning extra money.

$ The shoes in the window are saying 'BUY ME, BUY ME!'. You say, 'Yes, you are oh-so-pretty and you would look great on my feet, but that is not how I am going to choose to spend my money today. I am saving up to _____.' Or, 'All my extra money is going towards _____.' You fill in the blank.

$ Your child: 'I want _____'. You: 'Do you want that or do you want to go to Hawaii?' This is a real-life example and for 18 months, all three children chose Hawaii every time! **EVERY TIME!** It was an amazing family vacation and they learned a great lesson. **HONOR YOUR INTEGRITY**, it works!

Building a Wealthy Life is like building a house....

You have to start with a good foundation.

$+

HONOR
YOUR
INTEGRITY

HONOR YOUR INTEGRITY

The Way to Building a Solid Foundation

$ **Your Budget (The Plan) must = Your Values**

$ **Making Daily Decisions with Your Money**

$ **Goal Setting**

$ **Focus and Action**

$ **Behave As If**

$ **The Journey**

HONOR YOUR INTEGRITY

Your BUDGET (The Plan) must = Your VALUES

Remember this exercise?

As you create and review your **BUDGET**, keep your **VALUES** in mind.

For example, if you are currently renting but want to own a house some day, then honoring your **VALUES** means that your **BUDGET** needs to have a positive balance. You must pay off all consumer debt and accumulate **NO MORE** so that you can receive the best interest rate and decrease your stress level. You must save for a 20% down payment so you can purchase a home that you can comfortably afford. You must BUDGET, TRACK, and RECONCILE your financial information on a regular basis.

In short, you **BUILD A SOLID FINANCIAL FOUNDATION** by **HONORING YOUR INTEGRITY** with your **DAILY DECISIONS** and **ACTIONS**.

HOW TO BUILD A FINANCIAL FOUNDATION

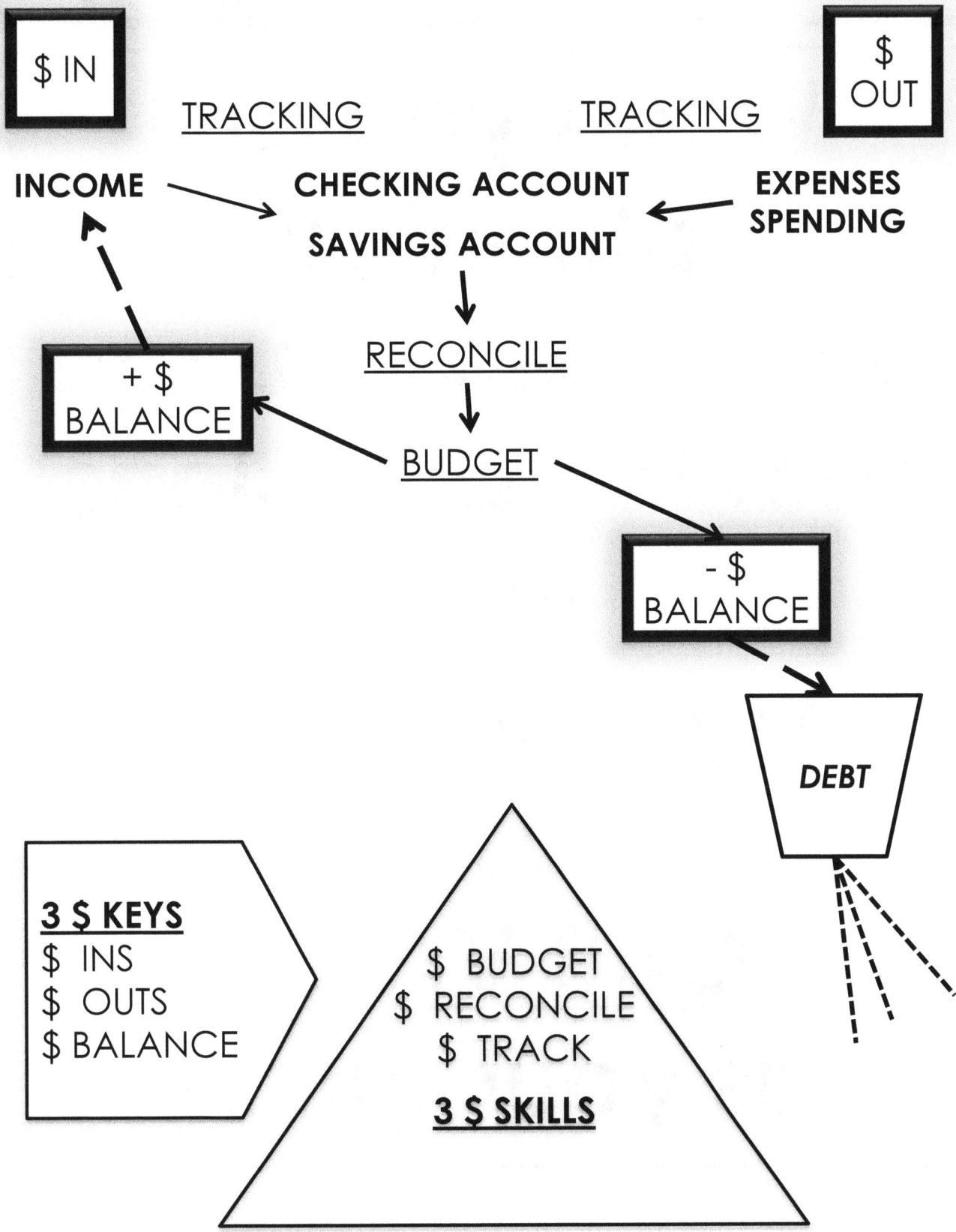

$ IN

$ OUT

TRACKING   TRACKING

INCOME   →   CHECKING ACCOUNT   ←   EXPENSES
                                              SPENDING
               SAVINGS ACCOUNT

+ $
BALANCE

RECONCILE

↓

BUDGET

- $
BALANCE

DEBT

3 $ KEYS
$ INS
$ OUTS
$ BALANCE

$ BUDGET
$ RECONCILE
$ TRACK

3 $ SKILLS

Honor Your Integrity

When you are
planning
and when you are
making decisions
with
YOUR MONEY,
use
YOUR VALUES
as your guide

HONOR YOUR INTEGRITY

Making Daily Decisions with Your Money

Decisions and Actions
make up our everyday lives.

Buy cute new shoes or pay off the credit card? Get dinner out or save for that down payment? Coffee or vacation? New furniture or a new car? Fancy electronics or an education?

Just as you cannot be in two places at once, you cannot spend your money on 'stuff' and expect to create wealth. You must consistently choose, over and over again. In order to create the desired outcome, you must make the decisions and take the actions that support the outcome that you **VALUE**.

It really is that simple, but sometimes it really can be that difficult.

When you don't HONOR YOUR INTEGRITY, you really are stealing from yourself.

HONOR YOUR INTEGRITY

Making Daily Decisions with Your Money

Decisions and Actions make up our daily lives. Here are some ideas to help you with your Daily Decisions with Your Money:

$ If you can't eat it, you don't need it (all we really need are the basics)

$ There are no sacred items

$ If you can't pay cash for it, you can't afford it

$ Up your income and plug the leaks in your expenses

$ Pay yourself first (save for what you want)

$ What to do with 'extra' money: pay off debt, up emergency fund, save for long-term or short-term goals

$ Focus on what you can control and change

EVERY DAY WE TAKE 100 LITTLE STEPS.
IN WHAT DIRECTION ARE YOU GOING?

Decision Making with Money

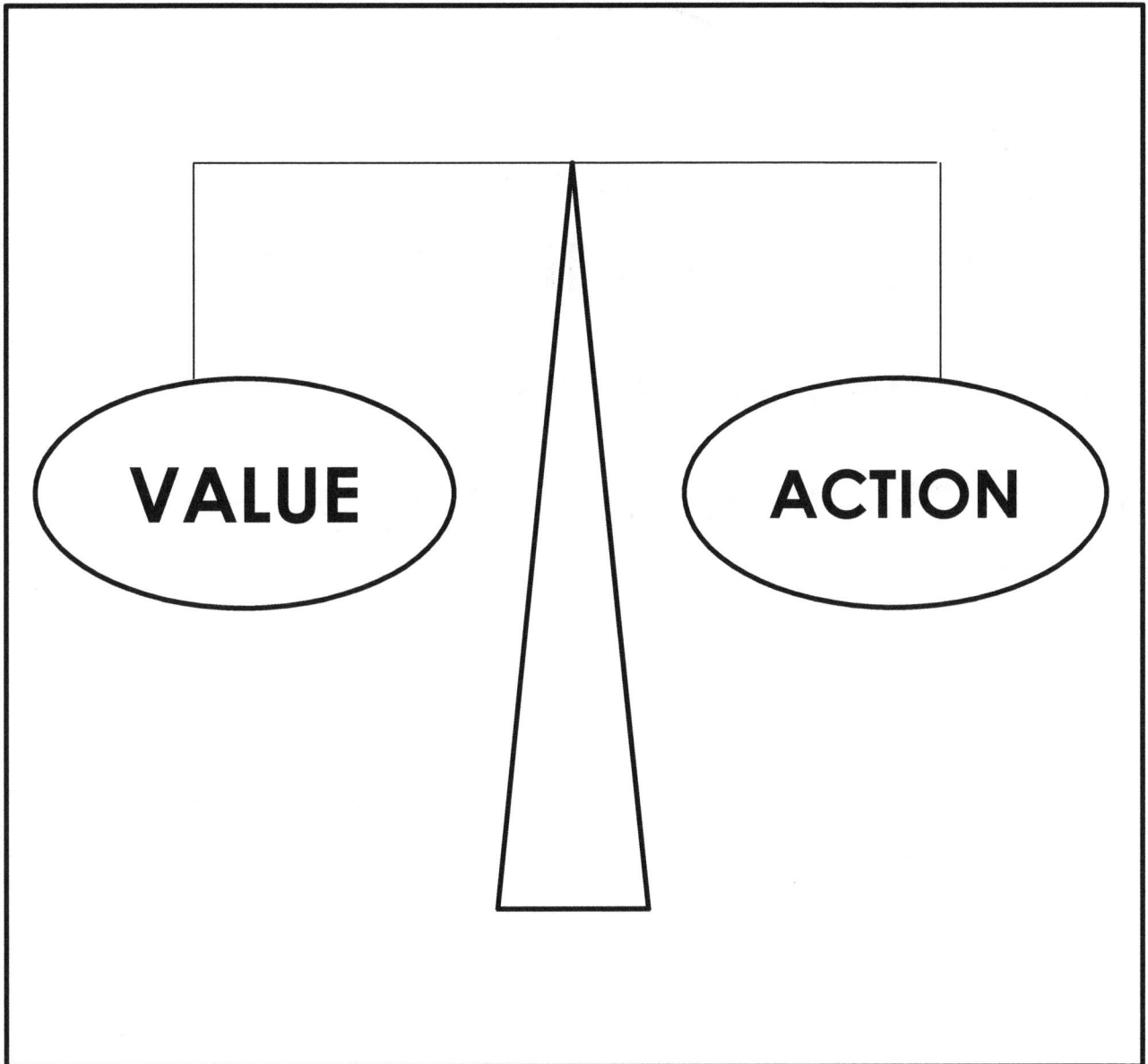

VALUE

ACTION

The Goal = The Direction

The Plan = The How

The Strategy = The Action

$⁺

HONOR
YOUR
INTEGRITY

HONOR YOUR INTEGRITY

Goal Setting

When you know what you **VALUE**, then you can set **GOALS**.

GOAL: 'An area toward which a player directs their efforts in order to advance' (The Direction).

I very much like this definition. It is playful! You are starting from where you are now and you **VALUE** advancement towards a new area (going in a certain DIRECTION).

You are in debt, you **VALUE** the act of getting out of debt. You have no emergency fund, you **VALUE** making an emergency fund. You have no retirement fund, you **VALUE** building a retirement fund.

So, THE GOAL is 'The Direction', THE PLAN is 'How you are going to get there', and THE STRATEGY is 'The daily Action and Decisions you make'.

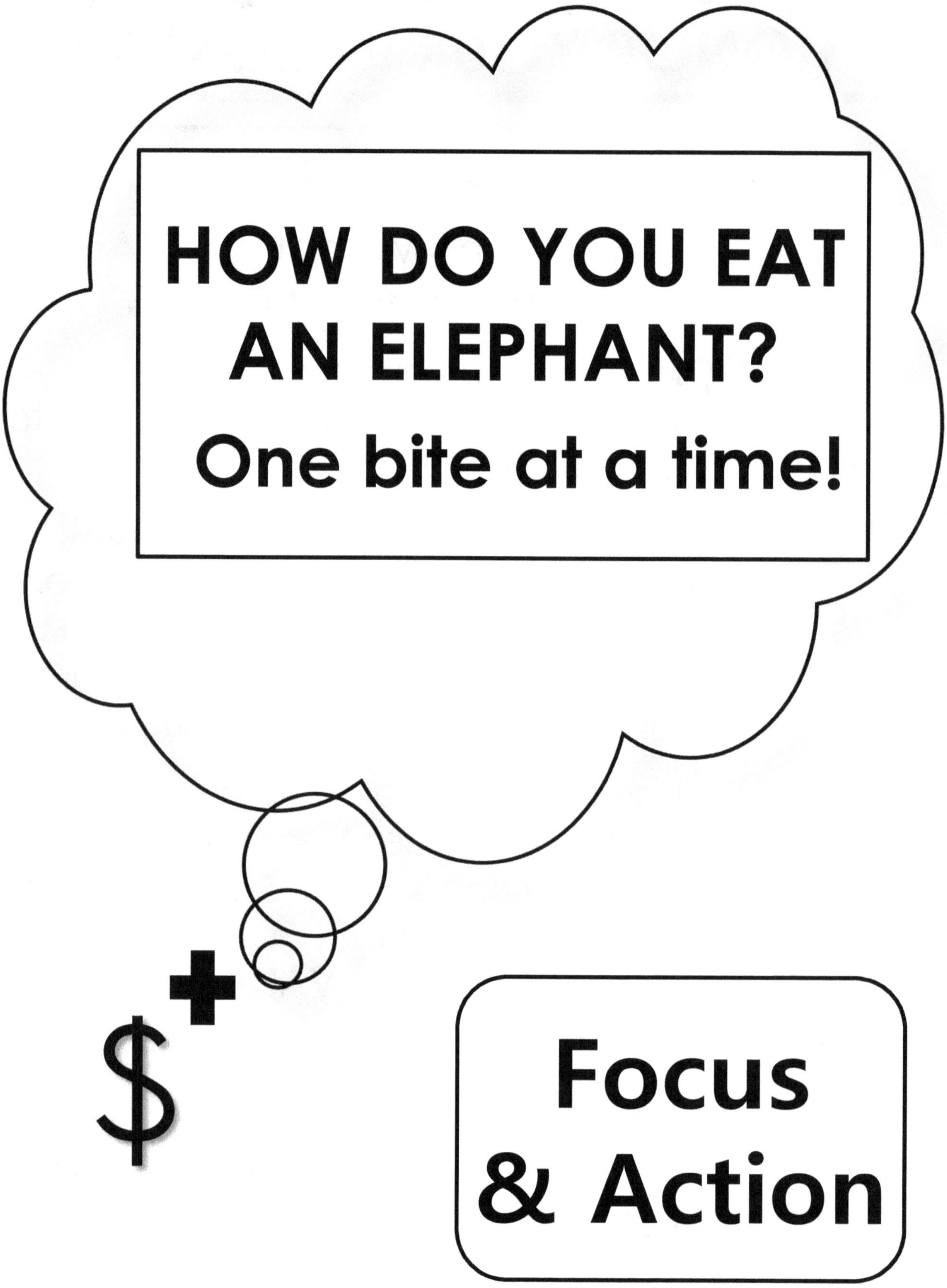

Focus & Action

Honor Your Integrity

FOCUS/ACTION

$ **Start from where you are NOW**

$ **Take small steps everyday toward your GOALS**

$ **Stay FOCUSED!**

Keep your eye on the prize. Sometimes, the road will get a little rough; go back to **Your VALUES, Your PLAN, Your GOALS**! Sometimes, you will think you are lost; go back to **Your VALUES, Your PLAN, Your GOALS**!

FOCUS…
This is an "F" word that you will want to use a lot!!!!

FOCUS/ACTION

Boys and girls, guys and gals,
Yoda had it right:

"There is no 'Try'".

'Try' is code for: 'I don't think I can' or 'I don't want to'.

Either way, go back and look at your **BELIEFS** or your **VALUES**. You may uncover a hidden **BELIEF** from your childhood or culture. You may discover that you have substituted someone else's **VALUE** for your own. Here again, this could come from family or culture.

Either way, this is part of **BUILDING A STRONG FINANCIAL FOUNDATION**. This is not a setback, but a great and powerful success in **HONORING YOUR INTEGRITY**.

Try Not!
Do, or Do Not.
There is No Try.

~ Yoda ~

$⁺

Focus
& Action

Behave As If

This is where you really start to empower yourself.

Culturally, this concept has been misused. So let me be clear. This does not mean to do/buy everything that you imagine you will do/buy when you have created your Wealthy Life. This is NOT a prescription to play now and pay later. NO, NO, NO. This is a mandate that you **HONOR Your INTEGRITY** regardless of whether or not you 'feel' like it, and regardless of how uncomfortable you 'feel', because it is a new habit.

Wealthy people have a plan. They take action based on that plan and they stay focused. So you are going to **Behave As If** you are a Wealthy Person right here, right now.

The next time you are tempted to 'blow the budget', I want you to stand up straight, throw your shoulders back, lift your head high, and proclaim, **'THAT IS NOT HOW I AM GOING TO CHOOSE TO SPEND MY MONEY!'**

That is NOT how I am going to choose to spend my money.

$\$^+$

Behave As If

THE JOURNEY

You are **Building a Financial Foundation**. This is a journey, a process. It does not happen overnight, and it never ends. If there was a 'magic' pill to just make it happen, I'd be on an island somewhere making 'magic' financial pills and selling them to you all. But there ain't, so here we are. The truth is that **WEALTHY LIVING** is like gravity. Gravity applies to everyone in the same way. No exceptions. **Wealthy Living** applies to everyone in the same way. No exceptions. Example: if you earn $10 and spend $8, you will have $2 leftover. If you earn $10 and spend $12, you will owe $2. This applies to everybody in the same way. No exceptions! You cannot violate the 'laws' of **Wealthy Living** and expect to **Live Wealthy**. What you can do is enjoy the journey and keep yourself well equipped for the ride.

Here are a few **Tools for your Toolbox** to help you along the way.

EVERY DAY WE TAKE
100 LITTLE STEPS...
IN WHAT DIRECTION
ARE YOU GOING?

$$^+

Other Tools
For Your
Toolbox

Tools for Your Toolbox

SELF CARE

Balanced Life

Exercise

Eat

Sleep

Relax

H.A.L.T.

Tools for Your Toolbox

Self Care

$ Balanced Life: Work hard, play hard

$ Exercise: Take care of your body

$ Eat: Feed your body healthy food

$ Sleep: Get a good night sleep

$ Relax: Rest, relax

$ H.A.L.T.: Hungry, Angry, Lonely, Tired. Stop (halt) and fix the problem. Do not make decisions or take action when you are Hungry, Angry, Lonely, or Tired.

Halt and take care of yourself.

Tools for Your Toolbox

Traits of Success

Watch or read about people that you truly respect. Make a list of traits/behaviors that lead them to their success. Then, **Behave As if**.

Here is one to get you started:

$ **Confidence/Courage**

$ **Curiosity**

$ **Opportunity**

$ **Plan**

$ **Action/Focus**

$ **Support**

$ **Humor**

$ **Service**

Tools for Your Toolbox

Traits of Success

$ **Confidence/Courage**: Faith or belief that you will act in a proper or effective way

$ **Curiosity**: Desire to know, to learn. Seek information, ask questions, seek out experts, develop good listening skills, and reflect

$ **Opportunity**: See opportunity in every situation

$ **Plan**: You have this one down by now

$ **Action/Focus**: This one too

$ **Support**: The team you surround yourself with, and how you take care of yourself. It is OK to ask for help, and seek out the best

$ **Humor**: Be childlike but never childish (see next page)

$ **Service**: Every person can be of service. The simplest act of service is to show up and do your best! If every person did this, the world would be awesome!

Honor Your Integrity

HUMOR

Laugh at yourself
Stay light
Stay positive
Build Confidence
Play
Be childlike

It's fun being you!
Enjoy the ride!

I am here for a purpose
and that purpose is to grow into a mountain,
not to shrink to a grain of sand.
Henceforth will I apply ALL my efforts
to become the highest mountain of all
and I will strain my potential
until it cries for mercy.

~Og Mandino

$⁺

BE BIG

WEALTHY LIVING

Is an individualized expression that is driven from your internal values

~ HONOR YOUR INTEGRITY

WEALTHY LIVING

Integrity does not consist of loyalty to your impulses but loyalty to your values.

Integrity requires long term thinking.

~ HONOR YOUR INTEGRITY

WEALTHY LIVING

TEAR-OUT PAGES

FOR

PRACTICE, PRACTICE,

PRACTICE

AND

FOCUS, FOCUS, FOCUS

EXPLORE YOUR BELIEFS

WHAT YOU BELIEVE DRIVES WHAT YOU THINK AND WHAT YOU THINK DRIVES HOW YOU BEHAVE

HOW TO BUILD A FINANCIAL FOUNDATION

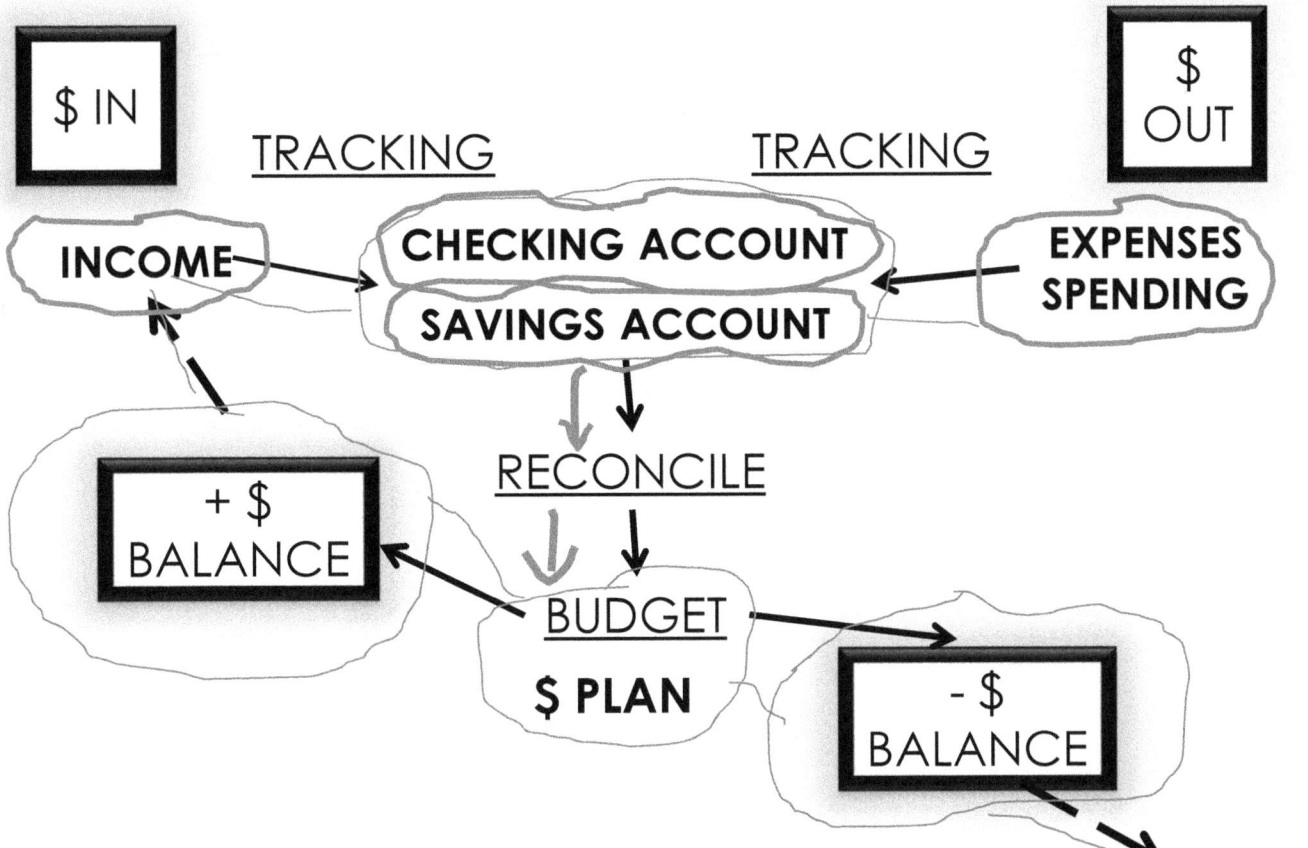

$ IN

$ OUT

TRACKING   TRACKING

INCOME

CHECKING ACCOUNT

SAVINGS ACCOUNT

EXPENSES
SPENDING

RECONCILE

+ $
BALANCE

BUDGET

$ PLAN

- $
BALANCE

DEBT

3 $ KEYS
$ INS
$ OUTS
$ BALANCE

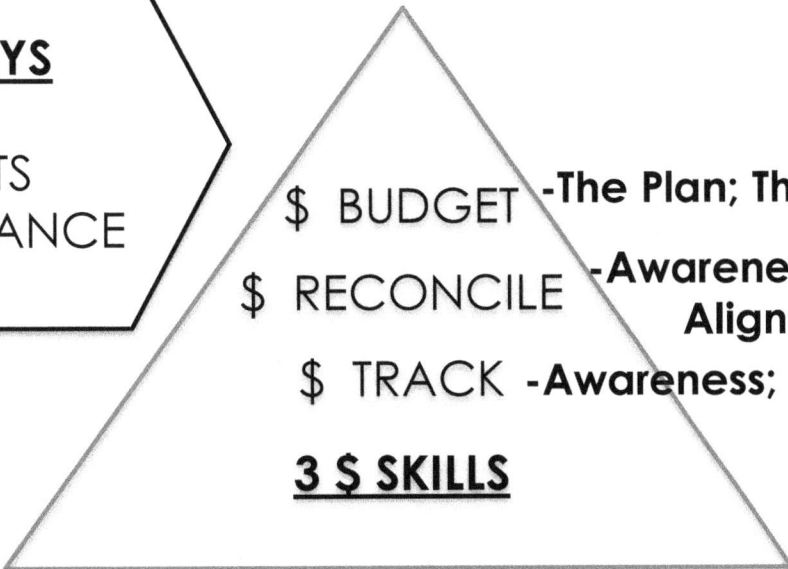

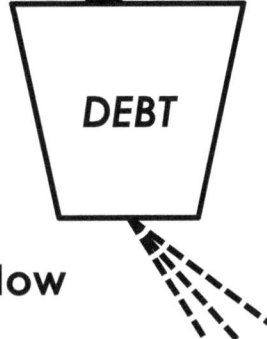

$ BUDGET -The Plan; The How

$ RECONCILE -Awareness; Attention;
Alignment

$ TRACK -Awareness; Attention

3 $ SKILLS

**RECONCILE ACTUAL NUMBERS
TO BUDGET NUMBERS.........**

Skills To Master

$ **Daily** – Track Expenses

$ **Monthly** – Balance Checkbook

$ **Monthly** – Reconcile Actual Spending

to Budget

$ **Every three months** – Adjust Budget Estimates

$ **Get Income Up**

$ **Eliminate or Reduce Expenses/Spending**

$ **Yearly** – Review Year

and Create New Budget

$ **As Needed** – Seek Help

$ **As Needed** – Celebrate Successes

DEVELOP YOUR SKILLS

Provided you maintain the conditions which make it possible, you can create anything

Including a financially fantastic life

INDIVIDUALIZED EXPRESSION

Don't trip yourself up on the 'Hollywood' version of Wealth

KNOW WHAT <u>YOU</u> VALUE

HONOR YOUR INTEGRITY

When you are planning and when you are making decisions with **YOUR MONEY,** use **YOUR VALUES** as your guide

WEALTHY LIVING

APPENDIX

Appendix 1

Investments
Rental Property
Taxes
Why this stuff isn't in the workbook:

As I created this workbook, I had many people provide input (some solicited and some not so much). The above were the most common items that came up as things that 'should' be in the workbook because 'this is what you need to be wealthy'. After contemplating the inclusion of these items, the following phrase overtook me. This workbook provides 'Tools' not 'Rules' for Wealthy Living. Yes, along the way you will want to develop new skills in the area of investing, you may or may not want to own rental property (it is not for everyone), and, well, taxes (enough said). But **FIRST**, you will need to **EXPLORE YOUR BELIEFS, DEVELOP YOUR SKILLS, CLARIFY YOUR VALUES,** and **HONOR YOUR INTEGRITY.** This will give you the foundation you need to explore these other areas. When needed, find great professionals that listen to you and **NEVER** substitute someone else's **VALUES** for your own.

Appendix 2

To Comingle or not to Comingle Funds? That is the Question

Here again, 'Tools' not 'Rules'. I wish I could give you some hard, fast checklist that would make this decision super easy, but, unfortunately, I cannot. Here are a few things to consider:

$ Second Marriages

$ Past Behavior – a bad track record is not going to instantly change overnight; it requires a lot of work. You cannot love someone out of bad habits.

$ Your Gut – if your gut tells you that there is an issue, believe it.

Always discuss financial beliefs, skills, and values and watch how your partner-to-be handles money. This is the second most intimate part of your relationship.

Don't ignore warning signs. Seek help with your partner as soon as possible. If they won't go, go by yourself. Ignoring a problem never makes it go away. **NEVER** substitute someone else's **VALUES** for your own.

Appendix 3

Statement of Net Worth ~ Your Score Card

Annually, add up all that you own (assets) and subtract all that you owe (liabilities). This is your **Net Worth.** Then set goals for how and by how much you want to grow your **Net Worth** each year. Example: Grow current investments by 8% ($10,000 @ 8% growth = $10,000 investment plus $800 growth = $10,800=**Net Worth** would increase by $800), increase contributions by $500 per pay check ($500 per pay check times 26 pay checks = $13,000 additional **Net Worth**). Want to make extra payments to the mortgage? What is your ultimate goal? One Million **Net Worth**, Two Million **Net Worth**? Remember, if you have $2,000,000 in investments and that money earns 10% per year, that = $200,000 of income per year. What does your retirement budget look like? How much money do you want to have to live off of each year?

Note, 'stuff' does not have much value in **Net Worth.** So unless you own something that can be sold for real value on the open market (say a signed, authenticated Picasso), don't include it. Many people are surprised that the crystal vase that grandma said was priceless doesn't fetch more than $30 on e-bay, or that the boat they paid $20,000 for sells five years later at $5,000.

Appendix 3a

What I Own:

House	+	
401(k)	+	
IRA	+	
Roth IRA	+	
Investments	+	
Kid's College Funds	+	
Money Market	+	
CD's	+	
Savings	+	
Cash	+	
Gold/Silver Jewerly	+	

What I Owe:

Mortgage	-	
2nd Mortgage	-	
Car Loans	-	
Credit Cards	-	
Student Loans	-	
Line of Credit	-	
Taxes	-	
Total:	**+ or -**	

NET WORTH

Notice how **Debt** eats all of your hard work. You can save & save & save, but **Debt** depletes all that work. You may add your car/s into your **Net Worth,** but be realistic about what you would receive for this kind of asset.

Appendix 4

Time Value of Money ~ Your Friend

INVESTMENT @:   **10%**   **+ $1/year**

Years	Beginning of Year Total Investment	Interest Earned	End of Year Total Investment
1	$1.00	$0.10	$1.10
2	$2.10	$0.21	$2.31
3	$3.31	$0.33	$3.64
4	$4.64	$0.46	$5.11
5	$6.11	$0.61	$6.72
6	$7.72	$0.77	$8.49
7	$9.49	$0.95	$10.44
8	$11.44	$1.14	$12.58
9	$13.58	$1.36	$14.94
10	$15.94	$1.59	$17.53

$ The schedules in Appendix 4 and Appendix 4a show both the time value of $1 invested per year and the total cost of $1 of debt per year.

$ Note, the total cost of $1 of debt = the cost of the debt **PLUS** the loss of investing the $1.

$ You can use this schedule for quick calculations. For every zero you add just add that number of zeros onto the end of the number and move the decimal point to the right by the same number of zeros added. (So, $1 to $100 dollars = add two 0's and move the decimal point to the right two spaces.) So at the end of year 10 at $100/year your investment would be worth $1,753.00.

Appendix 4a

Time Value of Money ~ Your Friend

DEBT @: 20% + $1/year

Years	Beginning of Year Total Debt	Interest Paid	End of Year Total Debt	The Loss of Investment	Total Cost of Debt
1	($1.00)	($0.20)	($1.20)	($1.10)	($2.30)
2	($2.20)	($0.44)	($2.64)	($2.31)	($4.95)
3	($3.64)	($0.73)	($4.37)	($3.64)	($8.01)
4	($5.37)	($1.07)	($6.44)	($5.11)	($11.55)
5	($7.44)	($1.49)	($8.93)	($6.72)	($15.65)
6	($9.93)	($1.99)	($11.92)	($8.49)	($20.40)
7	($12.92)	($2.58)	($15.50)	($10.44)	($25.93)
8	($16.50)	($3.30)	($19.80)	($12.58)	($32.38)
9	($20.80)	($4.16)	($24.96)	($14.94)	($39.90)
10	($25.96)	($5.19)	($31.15)	($17.53)	($48.68)

$ The schedules in Appendix 4 and Appendix 4a show both the time value of $1 invested per year and the total cost of $1 of debt per year.

$ Note, the total cost of $1 of debt = the cost of the debt **PLUS** the loss of investing the $1.

$ You can use this schedule for quick calculations. For every zero you add just add that number of zeros onto the end of the number and move the decimal point to the right by the same number of zeros added. (So, $1 to $100 dollars = add two 0's and move the decimal point to the right two spaces.) So an additional $100 of debt per year **COSTS** you a total of $4,868.00 over 10 years.

Appendix 5

Debt Pay-Off Schedule
~ Seeing How Every Penny Counts~

Debt 1

Principal Balance:	$1,000.00
Interest Rate:	10%
Payment:	$100.00

	Beginning Bal.	Principal	Interest	Ending Bal.
1	$1,000.00	($91.67)	$8.33	$908.33
2	$908.33	($92.43)	$7.57	$815.90
3	$815.90	($93.20)	$6.80	$722.70
4	$722.70	($93.98)	$6.02	$628.72
5	$628.72	($94.76)	$5.24	$533.96
6	$533.96	($95.55)	$4.45	$438.41
7	$438.41	($96.35)	$3.65	$342.07
8	$342.07	($97.15)	$2.85	$244.92
9	$244.92	($97.96)	$2.04	$146.96
10	$146.96	($98.78)	$1.22	$48.18
11	$48.18	($48.18)	$0.00	$0.00
TOTAL		$1,000.00	$48.18	$1,048.18

Appendix 5

Debt Pay-Off Schedule
~ Seeing How Every Penny Counts~

$ The interest in annual:
1,000 x .10 = 100 /12 (months) = $8.33 per month.

$ The $100 payment has two parts: one part pays off the interest that is charged for the month; the other part pays down the amount owed.

$ Next month's interest is calculated on the outstanding balance.

$ In this example, it will take 10 payments of $100 and an 11th payment of $48 to pay-off this debt.

$ The total cost of the item purchased is $1,048.

Appendix 5a

Debt Pay-Off Schedule
~ Seeing How Every Penny Counts~

Debt 1

Principal Balance:	$1,000.00
Interest Rate:	10%
Payment:	$110.00

	Beginning Bal.	Principal	Interest	Ending Bal.
1	$1,000.00	($101.67)	$8.33	$898.33
2	$898.33	($102.51)	$7.49	$795.82
3	$795.82	($103.37)	$6.63	$692.45
4	$692.45	($104.23)	$5.77	$588.22
5	$588.22	($105.10)	$4.90	$483.12
6	$483.12	($105.97)	$4.03	$377.15
7	$377.15	($106.86)	$3.14	$270.29
8	$270.29	($107.75)	$2.25	$162.54
9	$162.54	($108.65)	$1.35	$53.90
10	$53.90	($53.90)	$0.00	$0.00
TOTAL		$1,000.00	$43.90	**$1,043.90**

Appendix 5a

Debt Pay-Off Schedule
~ Seeing How Every Penny Counts~

$In this example the only thing that changed is the monthly payment.

$ An extra $10 per month is being paid. ($110 instead of $100)

$ The total cost of the item purchased is $1,043. This saves us $5 in interest, but it also does something else!

$ By making an extra $10 payment per month, the amount owed is paid off quicker.

$ In this example, it will take 9 payments of $110 and a 10th payment of $53 to pay off this debt.

$ This frees up $110 a month sooner to pay off other debts or to start saving.

Appendix 5b

Debt 2

Principal Balance:		$3,000.00
Interest Rate:		25%
Payment:		$100.00

	Beginning Bal.	Principal	Interest	Ending Bal.
1	$3,000.00	($37.50)	$62.50	$2,962.50
2	$2,962.50	($38.28)	$61.72	$2,924.22
3	$2,924.22	($39.08)	$60.92	$2,885.14
4	$2,885.14	($39.89)	$60.11	$2,845.25
5	$2,845.25	($40.72)	$59.28	$2,804.52
6	$2,804.52	($41.57)	$58.43	$2,762.95
7	$2,762.95	($42.44)	$57.56	$2,720.51
8	$2,720.51	($43.32)	$56.68	$2,677.19
9	$2,677.19	($44.23)	$55.77	$2,632.96
10	$2,632.96	($45.15)	$54.85	$2,587.82
11	$2,587.82	($46.09)	$53.91	$2,541.73
12	$2,541.73	($47.05)	$52.95	$2,494.68
13	$2,494.68	($48.03)	$51.97	$2,446.66
14	$2,446.66	($49.03)	$50.97	$2,397.63
15	$2,397.63	($50.05)	$49.95	$2,347.58
16	$2,347.58	($51.09)	$48.91	$2,296.49
17	$2,296.49	($52.16)	$47.84	$2,244.33
18	$2,244.33	($53.24)	$46.76	$2,191.09
19	$2,191.09	($54.35)	$45.65	$2,136.73
20	$2,136.73	($55.48)	$44.52	$2,081.25
21	$2,081.25	($56.64)	$43.36	$2,024.61
22	$2,024.61	($57.82)	$42.18	$1,966.79
23	$1,966.79	($59.03)	$40.97	$1,907.76
24	$1,907.76	($60.25)	$39.75	$1,847.51
25	$1,847.51	($61.51)	$38.49	$1,786.00
26	$1,786.00	($62.79)	$37.21	$1,723.21
27	$1,723.21	($64.10)	$35.90	$1,659.11
28	$1,659.11	($65.44)	$34.56	$1,593.67
29	$1,593.67	($66.80)	$33.20	$1,526.87
30	$1,526.87	($68.19)	$31.81	$1,458.68
31	$1,458.68	($69.61)	$30.39	$1,389.07
32	$1,389.07	($71.06)	$28.94	$1,318.01
33	$1,318.01	($72.54)	$27.46	$1,245.47
34	$1,245.47	($74.05)	$25.95	$1,171.42
35	$1,171.42	($75.60)	$24.40	$1,095.82
36	$1,095.82	($77.17)	$22.83	$1,018.65
37	$1,018.65	($78.78)	$21.22	$939.87
38	$939.87	($80.42)	$19.58	$859.45
39	$859.45	($82.09)	$17.91	$777.36
40	$777.36	($83.81)	$16.19	$693.55
41	$693.55	($85.55)	$14.45	$608.00
42	$608.00	($87.33)	$12.67	$520.67
43	$520.67	($89.15)	$10.85	$431.52
44	$431.52	($91.01)	$8.99	$340.51
45	$340.51	($92.91)	$7.09	$247.60
46	$247.60	($94.84)	$5.16	$152.76
47	$152.76	($96.82)	$3.18	$55.94
48	$55.94	($55.94)	$0.00	$0.00
		$3,000.00	$1,755.94	**$4,755.94**

Appendix 5c

Debt Pay-Off Schedule ~ Seeing How Every Penny Counts~

$ Looking at some bigger debt, you can really start to see what your debt costs you. $3,000 at 25% with a minimum payment of $100 will take you 4 years to pay-off, and the total cost is $4,755. That's $1,755 in interest charges.

$ Remember that it costs you even more than that! You lose the use of your $100 each month for 48 months plus the interest you could have been earning on your money.

$ As you can see, the finance companies understand the time value of money. Many of the companies make the minimum payments as low as possible to maximize the amount of interest you pay (and they earn!). With super low minimum payments, it takes you even longer to pay off your debt, and it costs you even more for your purchases.

$ The more money you apply to your debt (increasing the monthly payments), the quicker you will pay off your debt because the amount owed is paid off quicker. This also lowers the amount of interest you will pay in total.

$ Finally, remember that every time you take an extra $10 and buy some stuff, you could be applying that $10 to pay off your debt. If you buy stuff, you are stealing from yourself and your future.

$ So, every time you have that impulse to buy stuff or go out to eat, take that money and apply it to your debt.

~ Books and Stuff ~

I once heard Dr. Phil use the term 'target-rich environment'. That term really stuck with me. Placing yourself in a 'target-rich environment' will be helpful in building your strong financial foundation. Here are a few ideas:

$ Hang out with people who are good w/ their money. If you are going to 'copy' somebody, copy the person that is good w/ their money. Ask questions, shut your mouth, and hear what they say.

$ Just because somebody has stuff doesn't mean that they are good w/ their money.

$ Read about the HABITS of productive, successful people.

$ Go to the library and check out some personal finance magazines like *Kiplingers*. Learn new terms and how to do simple financial calculations.

$ Go online and use good, solid personal finance resources like Fidelity.com.

$ Don't give your money to someone just because they guarantee a great return. If it is too good to be true, it probably is.

$ Some of my favorite books: 'The 7 Habits of Highly Effective People' by Covey; and, 'Secrets of the Millionaire Mind' by Eker...READ, READ, READ!

$ TV Shows: 'The Suze Orman Show'; 'Til Debt Do Us Part'

$ Radio: Clark Howard; Local Personal Finance Show

~ Gratitude and Thanks ~

To my husband Matthew for teaching me how to trudge and for making ALL of our butterfly days come true. My parents Hurley and Judy for being my first teachers. Oh-so-many juicy girlfriends along the way: Nancy for recognizing the teacher in me; Renee for being my first 'client'; Jody, Karen, Susan and Dr. P for coaching me, holding my hand and giving me loving nudges when necessary. And for all the women and men who mirrored back to me what authentic ability looks like.

Dedicated to my children
Maddy, Jacq, and Jonathan.

You can do or be anything!
Your only limitation is
the roundness of the world.

About the Author

What imaginary games did you play when you were young?

Bethany played 'store', keeping ledgers of imaginary transactions of purchases and sales. Add this to a soul with a Bugs Bunny-like personality and the result is an accountant with a sense of humor.

Bethany holds two degrees. First, she has a PHD in the world's oldest profession. Yep, she's a housewife. Being completely comfortable with this title, Bethany understands the term 'economy' is Greek in origin (economos), and refers to a housewife shopping. The housewife is the most functional economist of all! – Making marginal decisions on the fly, based on her subjective values and resource constraint – trying to maximize the family's satisfaction from a fixed budget.

Bethany also obtained a B.S. in Accounting with a minor in Law and Economics. She worked for five years in public accounting as an auditor, and two years in corporate accounting. While homeschooling her three children, Bethany provided her accounting skills to several nonprofit organizations.

Her life's passion is to empower people through an understanding of simple financial and economic ideas and skills that will enable them to thrive financially. It is not the amount of money one earns, but what you do with it that really counts. When a person realizes they can create their own reality through mindful choice, that person is truly free. Bethany teaches that you must begin right where you are in the present moment. Then, you must take responsibility for your choices in making money, spending money, and saving money. You must create a healthy relationship with your money, and finally, stop pining for what you don't have but start enjoying what you do have.

When you recognize you have a choice, "I can't afford it" becomes "that's not how I choose to spend my money".

Choice and responsibility create freedom and power.

Bethany currently lives in Colorado with her husband and three children.

www.ingramcontent.com/pod-product-compliance
Lightning Source LLC
Chambersburg PA
CBHW080515090426
42734CB00015B/3062